Location-Based Social Media

'In this book Leighton Evans and Michael Saker declare that Location Based Social Networking is dead and loudly declare, 'long live LSBN'. As they explain, not only is there life left in LBSN and next generation location-aware social media, but they continue to raise important questions concerning the conception and use of space, time and identity. Drawing extensively on relevant literature, they provide a timely, fascinating and insightful analysis for those interested in understanding the full spectrum of social and spatial media.'

—Professor Rob Kitchin, *National University of Ireland Maynooth, Ireland*

'Evans and Saker do a strong job examining the social impacts of location-based social networks (LBSNs). They link LBSNs to a variety of topics, including embodiment, spatiality, and temporality, and they exhibit extensive knowledge of both the history of LBSNs and the current application environment. Most importantly, they write in a way that will remain relevant even as new LBSNs enter the market and our use location information shifts with even newer mobile technologies.'

—Jordan Frith, *Assistant Professor of Technical Communication, University of North Texas, United States*

'A highly readable and entertaining account of the life, death . . . and afterlife of location based social networking. This book provides a history of services that may soon be forgotten – who remembers Lovegety? But more than this Evans and Saker show that these may be responsible for shaping how we experience space, time and identity long into the future as features that once defined stand-alone location based services are mainstreamed into the social media giants.'

—Professor Susan Halford, *Faculty of Social and Human Sciences, University of Southampton, United Kingdom*

Leighton Evans • Michael Saker

Location-Based Social Media

Space, Time and Identity

Leighton Evans
University of Brighton
Brighton, United Kingdom

Michael Saker
Southampton Solent University
Southampton, Hampshire,
United Kingdom

ISBN 978-3-319-49471-5   ISBN 978-3-319-49472-2 (eBook)
DOI 10.1007/978-3-319-49472-2

Library of Congress Control Number: 2016961310

Cover illustration: Détail de la Tour Eiffel © nemesis2207/Fotolia.co.uk

Printed on acid-free paper

This Palgrave Macmillan imprint is published by Springer Nature
The registered company is Springer International Publishing AG
The registered company address is: Gewerbestrasse 11, 6330 Cham, Switzerland

To the 48% of people in the UK with some common sense

Acknowledgements

Leighton: While I do not wish to sound like a surprise Oscar winner, in any undertaking like this there are too many people to thank for helping in the completion of this work. I owe special thanks to my colleagues at the University of Brighton who have put up with some of my more articulate outbursts of frustration, especially Jackie Errigo, Holly Chard and Adrienne Rosen. Other thanks go to my colleagues Jo MacDonnell, Dario Linares, Helen Kennedy and my students who have often been useful sounding boards for ideas included in this book. The original proposal of this book was made possible while in receipt of funding from the European Research Council as part of the Programmable City project at Maynooth University (grant: ERC-2012-AdG 323636-SOFTCITY). My thanks go to Professor Rob Kitchin, and to the team at Maynooth who have offered support and advice. In particular, I thank Mark Boyle, Aoife Delaney, Robert Bradshaw, Sung-Yueh Perng, Tracey Lauriault, Chris Brunsdon, Martin Charlton, Paul Lewis, Conor Cahalane, Alan Moore, Darach MacDonncha, Jim White, Sophia Maalsen, Caspar Menkman, Claudio Coletta, Liam Heaphy, Orla Dunne, Melina Lawless and Rhona Bradshaw for maintaining order. Finally, thanks to Mike for making the co-writing of this book a pleasure, and Felicity Plester and Sophie Auld at Palgrave. Oh, and the folks, family and friends.

Michael: I owe a special thanks to all of my colleagues at Southampton Solent University, particularly Stuart Ray, Kieron Butler, Russell White, Tony Moon, Paul Rutter, Tony Steyger and Wez Nolan. Whether it be advice, support or simply being there, you have all helped me in countless ways that I am interminably grateful for. Other thanks go to Paul

Marchbank, Darren Kerr, Jamie Clarke and all of the students I have discussed the finer details of locative media with throughout my academic career. This book was made possible through a PhD Scholarship supported by the School of Social Sciences at the University of Southampton. I would consequently like to thank my supervisory team Pauline Leonard, Mark Weal and, especially, Susan Halford. Your exemplary supervision, relentless attention to detail and continued support means the world to me. Our time together remains a constant source of inspiration. I would like to thank all of my friends who have either helped me along the way or have provided levity and humour when I have needed it most. This thanks includes Pat Bond, Ryan Scott, Fatimah Awan and the incorrigible Mark Drury. I owe a huge thanks to my immediate and surrounding family, including Patricia Saker, Graham Saker, Chris Saker, Leona Saker, Ceara Saker, Katie Saker, Susan Varilly, Hugh Varilly, Owen Varilly, Vijaya Rudravajhala and Bill Howells (gone but never forgotten). Simply put, without you all this book would not be possible. I would like to thank Stephen Kennedy for inspiring me to take my studies further all those years ago, and for showing me what it means to actually teach. I would like to thank both Felicity Plester and Sophie Auld at Palgrave. A gargantuan thanks goes to Leighton for his unparalleled work ethic and for making the co-writing of this book an enormously satisfying experience – you genuinely are one of the good guys. A special and heartfelt thanks goes to my wonderful and talented wife for her unyielding support from day one. As always, you are my rock. Finally, an extra special thanks goes to my beautiful daughter Úna. What our relationship presently lacks in words, it more than makes up for in love.

CONTENTS

CHAPTER 1

Introduction

Abstract This introductory chapter offers a summary of the history of location-based social media networking (LBSN) and a review of some of the critical literature that has emerged in this area. The chapter draws attention to the historical precedents for recent, popular LBSN such as Foursquare and indicates where key features of historic LBSN have been retained in current services. As well as looking at the history of this media, the chapter begins to explore the 'death' of this media. The chapter also provides a detailed exegesis of the rest of the book.

Keywords Location-based social media networking (LBSN) · History of LBSN · Global positioning system (GPS) · Smartphones · Foursquare

This book is about those annoying status updates or tweets that tell you where someone is, with a tiny map of the location of that place and some comment by the user about that place and why they are there. At least, that is a very small part of what we are trying to cover. The activity of 'checking-in' and sharing location across a social network may be the most visible aspect of the use of location-based social networking (LBSN from here on) but the practices of use of this form of social media and the key structural and formal aspects of LBSN have now proliferated across social media. So, we are aiming to give some explanations not just about why

© The Author(s) 2017
L. Evans, M. Saker, *Location-Based Social Media*,
DOI 10.1007/978-3-319-49472-2_1

and how your friends and acquaintances on social media (and who knows, maybe you too) check-in using LBSN, but also how those LBSN platforms and services have become integrated into the monolithic social media platforms that dominate digitally mediated communications today, from Facebook and Twitter to WhatsApp (owned by Facebook, of course) and Yik Yak. While LBSN may have appeared marginal, they had a brief spell of immense cultural capital in digital media, and their impact has been profound in what we can do through social media and more importantly in how social media works to harness location as both a facilitator for information and a source of critical data about users. LBSN provided the blueprint for this, and the imprint of these services across social media is an important part of the legacy of these applications. In tracing the influence of LBSN on current media, we tell two interlinking stories: how LBSN carved a new niche of social media through its effects on spatiality, identity and temporality; and how LBSN applications and platforms failed to gain a critical mass of usage, but have permeated the social media landscape despite their perceived failure.

The second point (on the failure of LBSN) is reasonably controversial. Some advocates of LBSN may argue that these services still live, and are still popular. Foursquare still has 60 million registered users, and 50 million active users per month (Weber and Novet 2015) as of August 2015, and Foursquare and Yelp! have developed into location-search and location-ranking applications that have impacted on popular culture. The character Andre on FXX's *The League* often refers to his hipster use of Yelp!, and *South Park* parodied the Yelp! reviewer lifestyle in series 19, inspiring a bizarre meme/news story where it was rumoured that Yelp! was suing Matt Stone, Trey Parker and Comedy Central for $10 million (This Week 2015). Despite the continued presence of these services, LBSN applications are largely seen as a failure. Sixty million users are dwarfed by the billion-plus users of Facebook and the hundreds of millions of accounts on Twitter. The likes of Brightkite, Gowalla (bought by Facebook and closed), SCVNGR, Loopt, Sonar and Rummble have either fallen by the wayside and closed, or retooled and become other services in the digital economy. The influence of these services lives on in the functioning of the mobile platforms for Facebook, Twitter and other services. Neil Young once sang that 'it's better to burn out, than fade away'; LBSN burned out but never faded away, instead they have been folded into the fabric of the services that billions use on a daily basis. This book as the whole treats LBSN not only as a significant site of analysis but also as a form of 'dead' media that offers important insights into current and future social and digital media forms through analysis, inspired by (although not faithfully following 'down to the metal') the 'media archaeology' approach of Jussi Parikka, Erkki Huhtamo and others where close analysis of the trajectories and influence of obsolete media can inform analysis of contemporary media (although the obsolescence here is very recent).

This book offers an introduction to the history and use of LBSN, with four main points in mind. First, in this chapter we give a brief historical account of the development and uptake of LBSN, with a consideration of why so many LBSN didn't enjoy the mainstream success of other, more-established social media. Second, this leads to an overview of the 'death' of LBSN, as well as offering counterarguments that suggest that locative media is still used by a variety of users and communities, as it is being remediated in new forms such as Yik Yak or Facebook Places. This argument is threaded through this book and is the critical point of this book as a whole. Third, this book can be read as a literature review of the main academic approaches and work on LBSN, and how understanding of LBSN has come to inform understanding of other platforms and the behaviour of users, as well as how users' understanding of the world has been affected by LBSN use. Finally, the most critical aspect of this book is the three chapters that we contribute on the effects of LBSN use on spatiality, identity and temporality. The effects of LBSN on spatiality, identity and temporality for users of the applications have had profound and far-reaching influence on the use of social media, and we trace these developments throughout this book. In these chapters, we draw on the key literature developed on LBSN and ethnographic research with users of LBSN to illustrate how the use of LBSN has had specific and important effects on these facets of everyday existence and how these effects continue to reverberate through the use of digital and social media.

The remainder of this introduction is given over to a historical account of LBSN, providing information on early mobile social networking devices, such as Lovegety and Dodgeball (Humphreys 2007, 2010, 2013; Iwatani 1998; Reuter 1998), before moving on to more recent examples that provide the sites of research from which we draw our ethnographic material that informs the analysis in this book. This historical summary is intended to address the development of locative media, alongside the various affordances offered by different LBSN. This way of addressing the development of LBSN provides a historical snapshot of specific social media usage that is worthy of analysis due to the appropriation of LBSN features across other platforms. Close attention will be paid to the different effects these affordances can produce, as well as the different communities that still engage with locative media. The chapter concludes with an exegesis of the remainder of the book through a summary of the chapters and the main argument, that LBSN use plays a positive role in personal identity through its repositioning of the subject in space and the alteration of temporal aspects of spatiality to remediate identity through location and orientations to time.

1.1   THE DEVELOPMENT OF LBSN

The development of LBSN as social media platforms is not contingent on the emergence of social media platforms per se. The early matchmaking LBSN Lovegety, developed in Japan, first launched in 1998. This was a stand-alone device rather than application, and relied on the global positioning system (GPS) to match users with other available users in their vicinity. Rheingold (2002) remarked that this device was not only novel but also one of the first that involved a trade-off between privacy and the use of a service. Interestingly, the device retailed for around $21, a far cry from the 'free' services popular in the late 2000s and early 2010s. Of course, these services are far from free and are part of an explicit political economy of use where the labour of users checking-in to places is converted into advertising revenue (Evans 2013). The use of LBSN is also contingent on having an expensive, internet-connection-enabled smartphone with the obvious costs of such a device. Given the popularity of these devices though, the possibility of utilising their continual connectivity to the internet and embedded GPS units have allowed location-based services to be integrate into general, rather than specific devices. The transition to a 'mobile web' has given rise to new embodied experiences and social connections in space, through the use of applications dedicated to harnessing location and social ties. The use of smartphones and LBSN applications have allowed for the emergence of what De Souza e Silva (2006) referred to as a 'hybrid space'. This 'hybrid space' is a function of the combination of digital technology and physical spaces. With their digital, connected devices and location-based applications, users can interact with their location in a manner that moves beyond earlier mobile social networks. One of the first of these was Dodgeball (Humphreys 2007, 2010), developed by Dennis Crowley (who would eventually develop the later LBSN Foursquare) in 2000 before being taken over by Google in 2005. Dodgeball would eventually be shut down in 2009. Users would post their location on Dodgeball's accompanying website and it would send it out as a series of SMS text messages to a defined list of friends, patently not utilising the social network infrastructure nor efficiently using GPS systems in smartphones (coming slightly before the boom in these devices, and indeed shutting in light of not making efficient use of the technological developments in phones).

It is worth reflecting on the contingent nature of LBSN applications in light of this brief allusion to GPS. While the development of popular social networking platforms offered some formal aspects to the development of LBSN (think of the status update on Facebook or the tweet as the equivalent of the check-in) critically it is the technological affordances of smartphones that make these services possible. Before the advent of the smartphone, work-around solutions like bespoke devices or posting on the web before that post was relayed by SMS were the technological realities of LBSN. The explosion of popularity of the platforms of LBSN can be explicitly linked to the take up of smartphones following the launch of the iPhone in 2007 and the development of the alternative Android operating system and phones in its wake. These devices, enabled by embedded GPS and connectivity, afforded the development of the LBSN applications like Foursquare and Gowalla that are the focus of this book. So, the development of GPS and, in particular, the development of commercial applications of GPS for the civilian market has led to a new kind of information source on location, which has developed directly from innovations in commercial GPS devices. GPS devices require a database of places and geographical features to offer a functional user interface. While the databases used in GPS devices are proprietary ones, owned and controlled by the hardware manufacturers, databases in LBSN are largely created by the activities of users.

The social value of GPS embedded within mobile handsets, beyond mapping applications like Google Maps, became apparent at the South by Southwest (SXSW) music festival in January 2010. SXSW seemed to be a focal point for an emergent use of GPS in phones, tagging oneself to a venue or band playing at that venue. Membership numbers on Foursquare and Gowalla were exploding. This is possible through the technology embedded in what on first appearance are ostensibly phones: however, these are – in reality – miniaturised, sophisticated computers, or computational devices (Berry 2011, pp. 12, 14, 123). User-created content builds layers of information into maps and locational software. LBSN – Foursquare for example – build databases of places by users creating 'spots' and 'checking-in' at those spots. Foursquare launched on March 13th, 2009, and had 50 million registered users by May 2014 (Foursquare 2014). On Foursquare, users were (prior to an application redesign in

August 2014 that saw the check in function delegated to a new application called Swarm) rewarded in points-based systems for the creation of and checking-in to spots, and from this a game environment was created where users were encouraged to compete with friends for high scores over periods of time. Users were also rewarded with badges and titles for check-ins and creating spots: Foursquare did convey the status of 'mayor' on users who had the most check-ins at a spot. Users can still leave comments about spots they check-in at (and as many of these spots are services like restaurants or shops, this can be seen as a form of free advertising or user-review of the service) and photographs of the place. Links with other social networks, with Facebook and Twitter being ubiquitous options, help to find 'friends' and to post real-time updates to potentially larger audiences – all while promoting the application itself across other platforms (Evans 2015, pp. 37–38). When checking-in to a place, a list of nearby venues and places is automatically generated, providing the user with further information on their location and their relative position to other places and services. This founds the basis for the locational search function that has become critical to the mission and use of Foursquare since the initial excitement of its use in the early 2010s.

While the use of game design and gamification of location to attract and maintain users is interesting in these applications (see Saker and Evans 2016a) and something that will be expanded upon in the chapters that follow, it is the result of user activity that is more important to the actual development of the LBSN applications. Usage creates a user-created database of places, which is aided by other content such as comments and photos that adds a social dimension to the database. This development of the database of places requires an understanding of the development of the technological and computational elements that contribute to its realisation (Evans 2015, p. 40) which is why the device is so important in the analysis of LBSN in this book. To restate an obvious but important point: no smartphone, no LBSN, no user that sees a change in their understanding of spatiality, identity and temporality through their use of LBSN.

It is interesting to note how all these 'places' on LBSN are constructed. Typically, a user activates the application, which then quickly locates the user (or device, to be accurate) using GPS triangulation. This triangulated position is then matched up to spots that have been created nearby, for example a shop or restaurant. The users can check-in to these places (and leave a comment, or a photo, and post this check-in to another social network) or create a new spot. The spots are superimposed on a base map to insure accuracy. Initially, Google Maps were used for this purpose on many LBSN, but in February 2012 Foursquare moved to the Openstreetmap standard. Both Openstreetmap and Google Maps are indicative of a tile-based mapping technique that allows mapping applications to remain responsive while storing data through creating maps from a number of smaller tiled images (Sample and Ioup 2010, p. 2). When a place has been created, other users can also check-in at this spot, and information on check-ins will be relayed to friends of the user through a message to their mobile device. The really important part of this is the shift in production. Traditional maps made by organisations such as the Ordnance Survey in the United Kingdom and GPS systems such as TomTom operate in a top-down manner where the database is a created, closed system, without the interface for user contribution or editing. LBSN represent a bottom-up system, where the users of the application create the information held in the database. This open form of database is a contingent on users: some areas can be expected to have many spots, others none based on the relative facilities available and technological limitations (such as 3G coverage). In this sense, the device and LBSN is an exemplar of 'me-dia' (Merrin 2014, p. 1), where the application (facilitated by the device) focuses upon the individual in a hyper-localised manner. This means that the application is capable of providing and producing specific and hyper-relevant information as a form of horizontal, peer-to-peer and mediated interpersonal communication.

In this bottom-up form of database creation, businesses, venues and sites do not need to create their own entry on the database as a user will do this for them through creating a spot and checking-in to that spot. The political economy of this type of system is therefore quite advantageous to business, being built on free labour often without the consent of the business but more importantly without the labour of that business either (Evans 2013). With LBSN now concentrated on locational search, the presence of businesses and services on these platforms as created by users has obtained further significance. Take this example: if a place is created for a restaurant, a drinks manufacturer could directly advertise to a user within that restaurant that has checked-in there, or an offer on a meal could be made by the restaurant itself. The database stores data on individual users – where they go, when they go there and what they do in that place depending on the comments or annotations that a user contributes to the check-in. This is information that could be used to target the individual in the same way Facebook or Google collects data on usage to sell to advertisers. Barreneche (2012) argues that this classification, built upon an ontology of business-based vocabularies, is vital to an emerging form of economic governance of population mobility flows. In Barreneche's view, this mirrors a neoliberal urban politics of privatisation and the disappearance of public space.

In a previous book on LBSN, Evans (2015) outlined the development of the Ordinance Survey in the UK, arguing that mapping was a project that satisfied the political and economic wills of dominant elites within British society. This quintessentially top-down activity (enshrining the ownership of land in a formal representation of territory) stands in opposition to the kind of cartographic activity that we see with the use of LBSN. When one creates a place on Foursquare, there is not a top-down power relationship in the cartography. The creation of a gazetteer or database entry is both down to the users of the network (and therefore distributed rather than concentrated in the hands of a cartographer) and is immediately turned over to the network as a bottom-up (i.e. users creating the database rather than being 'given' the information) form of activity. Users can add to the map, and change the character of the gazetteers that have already been left on that map. In doing this, the user is actively involved in a transformation of physical space into social space, through the activity of mapping and navigating – the map is ontogenetic (Evans 2015, p. 87). The development of a database of places is indicative of a movement from (i) *representation of location* to (ii) *navigation of places* (Latour et al. 2010, p. 581), and a movement from Korzybski's notion of the map not representing territory to Siegert's (2011, p. 13) argument that maps can be considered as a space for representation in itself. These observations on the phenomena of the use of LBSN will be expanded upon later in this book, particularly in the chapter on spatiality.

In response to this new, user-driven activity which was highly visible across social networks and as part of the social media zeitgeist of the early 2010s a body of research now has developed concerning location-based applications (see Crawford and Goggin 2009; De Souza e Silva and Frith 2010; de Souza e Silva and Gordon 2011; De Souza e Silva and Sutko 2011; Evans 2015; Humphreys and Liao 2013; Wilken 2012, 2008; Wilken and Goggin 2012). Research in this field has explored how locative media are used to communicate and coordinate social interactions in public space (Campbell and Kwak 2011; De Souza e Silva and Sutko 2011; Humphreys and Liao 2013; Wilken 2008), leading to a continual sense of co-presence (Ling and Horst 2011; Rainie and Wellman 2012), affecting how people approach physical space (Campbell and Ling 2009;

Gordon et al. 2013; Martin 2014), turning ordinary life 'into a game' (Frith 2013; Licoppe and Inada 2008), and altering how mobile media is understood (Farman 2012). Accordingly, research has focused on the impact of LBSNs on space and place. As Humphreys and Liao (2013) have noted, '[one] of the goals of this area of research is to critically explore and understand the roles and impacts that mobile media have on individuals' everyday experience of place'. Frith's (2014) taxonomy of LBSN users (social users, gamers, explorers and cataloguers) is also critically important in the research cannon of LBSN. We identify roughly similar types of use, although elsewhere we have noted that players and explorers are often one and the same in our analysis of the 'playeur' (see Saker and Evans 2016a). The following chapters of this book will explore these themes through engagement with our own, original research with users of LBSN.

1.2 LOCATION-BASED SOCIAL MEDIA IN OUR OWN WORDS

Chapter 2 is concerned with the effects of LBSN use on spatiality, initially taking the form of a critical literature review that summarises the contestations on understanding the role of LBSN in approaching space and spatiality. This literature firstly attends to the spatial aspects of LBSN usage (De Lange and De Waal 2013; De Souza e Silva and Frith 2010; Erickson 2009; Evans 2014, 2015; Farman 2012; Frith 2012, 2013, 2014; Gordon et al. 2013; Humphreys and Liao 2013; Lindqvist et al. 2011; Martin 2014; Wilken and Goggin 2013), examining how LBSN have been shown to modify the routes people use to move through their environments (de Souza e Silva and Gordon 2011), producing new presentations of place (de Souza e Silva and Sutko 2011), and infusing ordinary life with a sense of play (Frith 2013; Licoppe and Innade 2008; Lindqvvist et al. 2011; Saker and Evans 2016a). The following discussion and analysis of spatiality draws on this existing research, but also will be grounded in established sociologically frameworks for approaching spatiality (De Certeau 1984; Lefebvre 1974/1991; Benjamin 1999) and city life (Simmel 1950). Earlier research on mobile phones and their impact on spatial coordination (Ling 2004; Ling and Yttri 2002) are also addressed in this discussion of the different approaches to spatiality LBSN enable. In taking this synoptic approach, the chapter acts as a comprehensive review of work on spatiality and LBSN, while also expanding upon previous conceptual frameworks to explain the spatial effects of LBSN use.

This chapter acts as a primer to research in the area, as well as addressing the following: a perspective on 'who' and what communities use LBSN and platforms to understanding location and space; how the 'spatiality' that is produced by the use of such socially constructed platforms is possibly exclusionary and elitist; and how the aspects of spatiality that emerge from LBSN have been integrated into other social media platforms, exploring why these have been seen as important in these platforms. This is done through drawing on ethnographic research with users of LBSN (including, but not limited to, Foursquare).

Chapter 3 is concerned with temporality and the effect of LBSN use on the perception and experience of time for users. LBSN carry a recursive function that offers a snapshot of previous check-ins at set time intervals, and the opportunity to review one's own check-in history. This chapter investigates why and how some LBSN users chose to archive their locational past and in doing so employed LBSN as a 'mediated memory object' (Van Dijck 2009). We explore the different ways that users interact with their preserved spatial past, a phenomenon that comes from the way that LBSN automatically archive users' spatial histories. We again offer an overview of the relationship between space and time as offered in the research literature (and how this theoretical work has influenced some of the work on locative media and LBSN) to set the ground for the analytical work in this chapter. The chapter then presents an analysis of the relationship between LBSN use, the marking and exploring of location and the temporal aspect of 'being-in a place' through a close engagement with phenomenological reflections on the relationship between technology and time. Here, we refer to how *technicity* (the role of technology in everyday life, Bradley and Armand 2006, p. 3) has a critical role in orienting humans to time (Stiegler 1998). In essence, technology (here, LBSN) in its use shapes the present as a phenomenological experience that brings forth the past in anticipation of the future in its usage. We argue that the temporal experience comes from an orientation to the future that allows the present to emerge. In the case of LBSN, as a particular object with a manner of orienting the user both in time and towards time, the present or now will be shaped in a manner commensurate with that nature.

What we are aiming to do in this chapter is to position LBSN as an archive, that then becomes a digital record that can be further furnished with images and text, following House and Churchill's observation that (2008, p. 300) '[a] visible shift in memory in recent years has been the increasing availability, sophistication, capacity and portability of con-sumer...capture/record technologies'. These changes have produced what Hoskins (2011) refers to as the 'connective turn', by which 'the formation of memory is increasingly *structured* by digital networks, [with] memory's constituting agency [being] both technological and human' (Van Dijck 2011, p. 402, emphasis added). In using LBSN, the present is restruc-tured by the projection of the event of checking-in into the future as a memory, and by past check-ins being recalled into the present. This duality of function marks LBSN as more than a mere modern technology, and as a particular memory-enabling device that has its own character thanks to its functioning. The remainder of this chapter will support this contention and add nuance to that character through an exploration of user experiences. The main focus of this chapter is therefore to uncover what the particular orienta-tion to time is as a result of LBSN use, through an engagement with user's experiences of LBSN and the manner in which the applications are used.

In Chapter 4, we draw the spatial and temporal elements of the work together, explaining how these components contribute to the personal identity of LBSN users, while underlining the lack of research in this area. The chapter begins by drawing parallels (and elucidating where features of each 'bleed into' the other) in LBSN use and the use of social networking sites (from this point on, SNSs) like Facebook, LinkedIn and Twitter. Research has indicated that 'self-presentation has moved from examining interpersonal interactions to displays through mass media' (Mendelson and Papacharissi 2010, p. 252). Work in this field has established that SNSs offer new 'front stage' ways for people to present themselves to others and '*keep a particular narrative going*' (Giddens 1991, p. 54; italics in original). Some individuals consider their identity and self-presentation as being akin to a 'brand', which they can then maintain through various sites (Cunningham 2013; Senft 2012). Our analysis looks to extend these insights to LBSN, and to explain the role of the understanding of space that comes through LBSN and the inorganic organisation of memory/ exteriorisation of memory and temporal alterations in spatiality that LBSN allow. Identity (as mediated by LBSN) is positioned as a performative act that is a product of considerations on both spatiality and temporality.

To do this we draw on established sociological frameworks (Goffman 1959) with regard to presentations of self. Following the grounding in SNS studies, we examine research that has provided a heuristic for examining identity and LBSN through the presentation of place (de Souza e Silva and Sutko 2011; Humphreys 2007, 2010). These early insights are then further developed with reference to Schwartz and Halegoua's (2014, p. 5) 'spatial self', which we use as a 'lens through which to read the myriad expressions and performances of identity and place online via social media'. Expanding upon the 'spatial self', the chapter explores two additional ways LBSN can be understood as affecting identity outside the sharing of location: the act of mediating the 'self' through LBSN and the use of locational suggestions (or location search). Underpinning these discussions is the idea that the role of locative media on identity should not be thought of as abstracted from spatiality and temporality. This chapter examines whether users of LBSN understand that using these applications are a way of presenting their identities across these and other platforms. The effects of LBSN use on spatiality and temporality reflected upon in the previous chapters' covalence into this remediation of identity, and the role and functioning of LBSN in other social networking platforms is again considered here in how the salient features of LBSN on personal identity contribute to identity formation and maintenance on other platforms.

Our final chapter reiterates the conclusions derived on spatiality, temporality and identity and considers these findings in the context of other research and theory in the area. We also survey the area of LBSN as it stands. Given the mainstream failure of stand-alone LBSN, but the increasing use of LBSN features in other popular social networks, this chapter will analyse both the shortcomings of LBSN applications and the reasons why their key functions are being retained and integrated into other platforms such as Facebook and Twitter. The conclusions of both this book and research in the area will be used to assess critically the nature of current LBSN in the context of how places, users and identity are represented, mediated and framed by the applications. In assessing the long-term effects of LBSN on other platforms, the functioning of locative media is related to the political economy of data production through locative applications, which provide rich data for targeted advertising. This political economy is related back to the findings of this work on identity, spatiality and temporality. The chapter will culminate in a series of suggestions on how future research on LBSN could proceed, and will expand on the view that while individual LBSN applications are disappearing, their architecture and functioning are becoming stable parts of other, bigger social networks. In doing so, the book underlines the importance of LBSN as a historical marker of social media's incorporation of the mobile web and location. LBSN and the research on them still matter and still will matter in the future.

CHAPTER 2

Space

Abstract This chapter offers a comprehensive summary of the research on LBSN and spatiality, building to a critical analysis of the effects of LBSN use on understanding the spaces around users through the mechanism of play. The chapter also draws attention to the spatial turn in the humanities and the importance of the shift in social theory from questions of time to questions of space through an exegesis of the work of Lefebvre, de Certeau and others. We interrogate the spatial effects of LBSN use as an instance of altered understanding of space and place through an examination of how playful uses of Foursquare have led users to understand their environments differently, which also implicitly questions long-held theoretical positions on play and spatiality.

Keywords Spatiality · Play · Spatial practices · Flâneur · Embodiment

2.1 Spatiality Isn't Just Lines on Paper...

Our approach to spatiality and the effect of LBSN use on spatiality follows a long-established shift in social theory 'from questions of temporality to those of spatiality' (Elden 2004, p. 189), although ironically we will reverse this shift somewhat in the next chapter to consider temporality. This chapter serves two purposes: firstly, to outline key research in the use of LBSN that has focussed upon spatiality; and secondly, to extrapolate our own views on the importance of LBSN to spatiality from our empirical

© The Author(s) 2017
L. Evans, M. Saker, *Location-Based Social Media*,
DOI 10.1007/978-3-319-49472-2_2

research. In tracing the spatial elements of LBSN use we are following the spatial turn in social theory, the impetus for which can be attributed to Lefebvre (1974/1991) and his insistence upon the importance of location. Through emphasising location, the possibility of critically interrogating the nature of space is opened up and implicitly there is a rejection of the Kantian notion of time and space as being simply a priori (independent of experience, unchanging and essential in nature) containers of experience. As Lefebvre (1974/1991, p. 2) explains, 'Kantian space, albeit relative, albeit a tool of knowledge, a means of classifying phenomena, was yet quite clearly separated (along with time) from the empirical sphere'. For Lefebvre, what Kant significantly failed to appreciate was the active character of space. 'No longer the Kantian empty formal containers, no longer categories of experience, time and space could be experienced *as such*, and their experience was directly related to the historical conditions they were experienced within' (Elden 2004, p. 185).

As Stuart Elden (2004, p. 187) explains, 'As early as 1939, Lefebvre had described geometric space as abstractive, and had likened it to clock time in its abstraction of the concrete'. This view is illustrated in Lefebvre's work *Descartes* (1947) where the Cartesian distinction between the ideal and the real was interrogated. For Descartes, according to this account, 'all problems can be reduced to the length of some straight lines, to the values of the roots of the equations, thereby turning space into something measurable' (Elden 2004, p. 187). The *experience* of space was elided in favour of the abstract representation of space in thought, under the auspices of scientific quantification. Lefebvre's (1974/1991) seminal work *The Production of Space* can accordingly be understood as an attempt to overcome the Cartesian divide between mental space and real or lived space.

> On the other hand, and following from this, space is a reality, outside of thought, the thought of the Cogito. Space is res *extensa* [(the physical world)], which is entirely other than *res cogitans* ([the thinking being]). This position is, of course, untenable. If space is an 'extended thing' entirely other than thought, then thought is unable to comprehend it; if space is nothing other than thought, knowledge of space is without content. (Elden 2004, p. 187)

Understanding space as either abstract or concrete was, for Lefebvre, paradoxical because it failed to account for the 'lived experience' of space. A similar view on this paradox can be found in De Certeau's (1984) thoughts from the 110th floor of the World Trade Center, as detailed in *The Practice of Everyday Life*. What struck de Certeau as he looked out across Manhattan was the image's failure to represent the lived experience of actually being 'down below'. 'When one goes up there, he leaves behind the mass that carries off and mixes up in itself any identity of authors or spectators' (De Certeau 1984, p. 92). What was apparent to De Certeau (1984, p. 94) was the problematic relationship between geometric and anthropologic space, the difference between 'the *concept* of a city' and the 'urban *fact*'. The '*concept* of a city' fails to appreciate the active role played by the individuals 'down below' in the construction of the spaces. For Buchanan (2000, p. 110) this means that 'the constellation of lives that make a city what it is . . . the actual experience of the city . . . is not contained in the concept of the city'. 'The *concept* of the city' as a geometric expression of space cannot represent the countless paths, stories and perspectives that are traced by the pedestrians that inhabited these spaces, forged at the street level.

Following de Certeau's inversion of traditional understandings of the terms space and place, where place refers to 'the order (of whatever kind) in accord with which elements are distributed in relationships of coexistence' (1984, p. 117), we draw our own distinction between the terms here and throughout the book. In our analysis of LBSN, we are less interested in the geometrics of the city (place) as we are interested in the use of LBSNs within the environment, and what effect use of these applications have on experience of space. As the primary focus in our analysis is the 'lived' experience of using LBSNs to understand the world, our focus is therefore in how space is understood and made through interactions with LBSN, with place referring to the labelled, stable identities of places in the environment. As de Certeau says: 'space is practiced place'.

Lefebvre (1991, p. 33) suggested that space should be understood in three overlapping ways: 'spatial practice, representations of space and representational space'. In this way Lefebvre understands space as simultaneously perceived, conceived and lived. As Elden (2004, p. 190) explains:

> The first of these takes space as physical form, *real* space, space that is generated and used. The second is space of *savoir* (knowledge) and logic, or maps, mathematics, of space as the instrumental space of social engineers and urban planners, of navigators and explorers. Space as a mental construct,

imagined space. The third sees space as produced and modified over time and through its use, spaces invested with symbolism and meaning, the space of *connaissance* (less formal or more local forms of knowledge), space as *real-and-imagined*.

To consider this suggestion through the eyes of de Certeau from atop the World Trade Center would produce the following view. The perceived space of Manhattan would be the city itself, in its vibrating and interminably evolving totality; the *real* space of the environment, if you will. The conceived space would be the abstracted cartographic map overlaying the streets and back alleys. Finally, the lived space would be the embodied experience of actually being within the city, of configuring oneself amongst the myriad flows and forces that emanate from 'down below'. De Certeau highlights the implicit somatic difference between experiencing the city from an abstracted position and actually being there. Lefebvre's 'representation space' illuminates the productive, or rather constructed, character of space as well as the phenomenology of actually interacting with a tangible environment. This is something not accounted for by either spatial practices or representations of space on their own.

A more embodied way of exploring the lived space of Lefebvre (1991), one that involves '[rewriting] spatiality in terms of perspective' (Buchanan 2000, p. 112), is through the Parisian figure and spatial practice documented by both Baudelaire (1964) and Benjamin (1999): the *flâneur*. *Flânerie* grew out of a specific time and place, specifically nineteenth-century Paris; a period which witnessed the construction of glass-covered arcades, creating an interior-without or rather an exterior-within (Geist 1983). As Benjamin (1999, p. 417) explains:

> Paris created the type of the flâneur...Paris [is] the Promised Land of the flâneur – the 'landscape built of sheer life', as Hofmannsthal once put it. Landscape – that, in fact, is what Paris becomes for the flâneur. Or, more precisely: the city splits for him into its dialectical poles. It opens up to him as a landscape, even as it closes around him as a room.

The art of *flânerie* involves moving through one's environment at an unhurried pace, just 'behind the fashionable amble of a pet tortoise' (Shields 1994, p. 65). This movement is not geared towards a specific destination but is instead focused on visually absorbing the urban surrounding as an aesthetic practice in its own right. As Tester (1994, p. 1) explains, 'the activity of strolling and looking which is carried out by the *flâneur*, is a recurring motif in the literature, sociology and art of urban, and most especially of the metropolitan, existence'. For Baudelaire (1964), the *flâneur* is a kind of poet that uses, modifies and appropriates the metropolis as a locational canvas to build upon, merge with and get lost in. The metropolis is a material to mould, texturise and clarify evoking the *lived* space of Lefebvre as well as the observed 'stories' of de Certeau as written by the pedestrians 'down below'. Indeed, for De Certeau (1984), this form of appropriation would be termed an 'art of doing'. To link this to embodiment, what this highlights are the various *ways* that space alters experiences and how experience alters space. This is important for our perspective on space in this book. Space can be reconfigured to produce different effects, patterns and understandings. This is significant as it means that the incorporation of LBSN in everyday life have the potential to produce new approaches to space, if space is constructed as opposed to given. In this chapter, we detail how use of LBSNs is a co-constituent in the production of new, embodied approaches to spaces.

This co-constitutive status of LBSN in the construction of spaces is a product of the functioning of these applications to relay location-specific data and information to users in real time. The overlaying of 'real' world environments with data and information is indicative of the movement of the internet itself from the desktop to what we now understand as the 'mobile web', the use of internet-based services and applications through continually connected smartphones and devices. 'The accessibility and mobility of these devices suggests that people can . . . connect with local people in real-time as they move through the cities' (Humphreys 2010, p. 764). A prime example of a service that does just this was explored by Humphreys (2007, 2010) in her study of the mobile social network, Dodgeball. Dodgeball was developed by Dennis Crowley (the future co-founder of Foursquare) in 2000, before being taken over by Google in 2005, and then eventually shutdown in 2009. During its tenure, Dodgeball functioned in the following way: users would post their location on Dodgeball's accompanying website which would then send out a series of SMS text messages to a defined list of friends, updating them of their whereabouts. From her research, Humphreys (2010, p. 768) found that using Dodgeball shaped how users felt about their environment, identifying a process termed 'parochialization'. Through 'creating, sharing and exchanging information, social and locational', users felt a 'sense of commonality among a group of friends in a public space'. This produced a sense of familiarity within often-unfamiliar public environments, and could lead to unexpected social interactions. Furthermore, Humphreys also found users frequently changed their pathways through the city depending on what social and spatial information they had received on their mobile devices; reconfiguring or adapting their usual routes if it became apparent that a friend or friends were nearby. These findings support the idea that '[people] increasingly use mobile social networks to transform the ways they come together and interact in public space' (Humphreys 2010, p. 764), and that the mobile phone can be 'firmly embedded in what it means to experience place, co-present or not' (Hjorth 2008, p. 93). The use of mobile phones to find ways around and find out about spaces therefore co-constructs a sense of space for that user.

Since Dodgeball, the mobile phone has moved way beyond SMS text messages in terms of its communicative potential. Smartphones, devices enabled with internet connectivity and a wealth of applications that can draw on location through GPS capabilities and the ability to draw on data from applications have become a familiar to many people in everyday life. The presence of these devices has altered the ways in which mobile phones are understood, and what they are 'for' (Ling and Pedersen 2005; Bassett 2003; Fortunati 2002). As Richardson (2007, p. 205) observes:

> Handheld media and communications technologies are becoming increasingly composite interfaces, combining the functionality of standard telephony, text-based interaction, e-mails and Internet browsing, digital video cameras, PDAs, MP3 players, and game consoles.

Boyd (2005, p. 28) describes these devices as 'the Swiss army knife of consumer electronics'. Hjorth (2008, p. 91) concurs:

> Whether we like it or not the mobile phone has become a vehicle for multimedia...so much so that users who just want a mobile phone for voice calls find it impossible to get such a device without all the 'extras'.

The significant feature of smartphones is that they allow users to access the web as they move, enabling 'real' world locations to be overlaid with digital information. Prior to this transition, 'surfing the net' necessitated minimal physical movement or spatial awareness; the 'computer [could] be said to discipline the body more or less into a face-to-face interaction'

(Hjorth 2008, p. 101). For De Souza e Silva (2006), this merging of 'real' world environments with digital space has led to the development of 'hybrid spaces'. Hybrid spaces produce a sense of 'virtual co-emplacement' (Moores 2006) and a doubling of space as users now inhabit two different spaces, the digital and the 'real', simultaneously. This concept forms an important part of the research surrounding new mobile technologies and location-based applications (Farman 2012; De Souza e Silva 2006). This 'hybrid' engagement involves more than interacting with digital information in space; interacting with digital information in space is related to a specific location in which that information is accessed and contextualised.

If space and experiences of space are understood as constructed through use, rather than being predetermined (Soja 1996; de Certeau 1984; Lefebvre 1974/1991), this means new approaches to space (alongside new social possibilities) could emerge from the use of LBSNs due to the 'hybrid' spatial engagements they create. In this chapter, we take this as the starting point but develop this further through engaging with the concept of embodiment. If embodiment can be understood as not limited by the body itself (Richardson 2005; Ihde 1993; Merleau-Ponty 1962, 1964) but rather open to alteration by the various technologies we employ as prosthesis then the use of smartphones to discover information on spaces may be considered an embodied activity. More on this later.

2.2 Research on LBSN and Spatiality

If we consider LBSN as software, then it is important to contextualise software as an element in spatiality. As a factor in the world, software shapes societal relations and economic processes through the automatic production of space (Thrift and French 2002) that generates new spatialities and the creation of software-sorted or machine-readable geographies that alter the nature of access and governance (how societies are organised and governed to fulfil certain aims; Graham 2005) (Dodge and Kitchin 2011, p. 7). Dodge and Kitchin argue that the effect of software (or code) on spatial understanding is to continually modify space; that is continually bring space into existence through processes of transduction that emerge from the functioning of code. Transduction in this instance refers to an operation in which a particular domain undergoes an 'ontogenetic modulation' (Mackenzie 2003, p. 10). This may seem like pure jargon, but the idea is fairly straightforward: ontogenesis refers to the origin of a domain coming into existence (Dodge and Kitchin 2004, p. 170). In the context of the use of computational devices, as an extension of the rules and instructions of software (code) continually shapes our understanding of space through our interactions with coded objects (such as smartphones) and technologies that bring spaces into existence (or awareness). The effect of these transductions is to create a series of 'coded practices' that are a combination of code and human practices that become a way of acting and being in the world, specifically in understanding and acting in spaces that undergo transductions.

Given the importance of these coded practices, we are interested in research on LBSN that has looked on the possibilities of opening up and creating new spatialities through the use of LBSN as coded practice. Analyses of the impact of location-based services have been numerous in consideration (Wilken 2012, p. 243), but some major areas of research have emerged. Wilken (2012, p. 243) identifies the major themes as research directed towards analysing how locative technologies mediate the relationship between technology use and physical or digital spaces (see Crawford and Goggin 2009; De Souza e Silva and Frith 2010; De Souza e Silva and Sutko 2011; Wilken 2008, 2011; Wilken and Goggin 2012), discussions of power and politics in location-based services (see Elmer 2010), and assessments and discussions on the nature of the repre-sentation of space that emerge through locative media (Gazzard 2011). In addition, the area of privacy has been a major area of interest (See Friedland and Sommer 2010; Michael and Michael 2009; Freni et al. 2010). A substantial body of research has developed on location-based applications (see Crawford and Goggin 2009; De Souza e Silva and Frith 2010; de Souza e Silva and Gordon 2011; De Souza e Silva and Sutko 2011; Evans 2015; Humphreys and Liao 2013; Wilken 2012, 2008; Wilken and Goggin 2012). Research in this field has explored how locative media are used to communicate and coordinate social interactions in public space (Campbell and Kwak 2011; De Souza e Silva and Sutko 2011; Humphreys and Liao 2013; Wilken 2008), leading to a persistent sense of co-presence (Licoppe 2004; Ling and Horst 2011; Rainie and Wellman 2012), affecting how people approach physical space (Gordon et al. 2013; Ling and Campbell 2009; Martin 2014), turning ordinary life 'into a game' (Frith 2013; Hjorth and Richardson 2014; Licoppe and Inada 2008) and pointedly altering how mobile media is understood (Farman 2012). As Humphreys and Liao (2013) have noted, '[one] of the goals of this area of research is to critically explore and understand the roles and impacts that mobile media have on individuals' everyday experience of place'. Accordingly, the research agenda on LBSN has focused on the impact of LBSNs on space and place. In the context of this chapter, it is research on the playful relationship between space and digital technology in which we are interested.

The body of research does support an idea that the use of mobile media alters the way that users relate to physical space in a convergence of location, digital networks and location-specific information that mediates geographic spaces (Martin 2014, p. 180; Campbell and Ling 2009; Gordon et al. 2013). The ubiquity of connectivity with mobile communications (Okazaki and Mendez 2013), the perpetual contact with social ties, the continual potential of accessibility of social ties that creates a continual co-presence (Ling and Horst 2011) and the possibility of instant interactivity with others (Campbell and Kwak 2011) are the features of mobile internet use that create the possibility and affordance of a transformation of the experience of space when using mobile media. Gordon et al. (2013) argue that location-based services mediate conceptions of space and geography while contributing to changes in understandings of participation in public life for users. The use of this technology does not detract from conversing with others in public space (Campbell and Kwak 2011, p. 207) and indeed can lead to more interaction as major events are relayed in real time to users in the same location. Hampton et al. (2010, p. 701) found that online activities in public spaces may contribute to higher overall levels of social engagement than in spaces where internet connectivity is not available.

As we've already alluded to, de Souza e Silva and Gordon's (2011) canonical work *Net Locality* assesses location-based services as technologies that open up hybrid realities between location and technology. A hybrid situation in this view is one where the local and the remote cannot be clearly defined as the mobile technology pulls in remote information to inform the situated actor in the local context. The presence, and more importantly use, of this information in local context has a transformative effect on the experience of space for the user. In short, the presence of the software transforms the experience of space. De Souza e Silva and Gordon's work encompasses the critical feature of contextual information available in real time thanks to continuous connectivity, and it is this that we focus upon in this chapter.

We've already mentioned Humphreys' (2005, 2008, 2010) work, which utilised ethnographic methods to suggest that people map their understanding of common social rules and dilemmas onto new technologies, and over time this creates a new social landscape. This kind of approach to understanding the mediation of space through media usage is indicative of what we attempt here. Humphreys (2010) argued that mobile social networking has the potential to transform the ways that people come together and interact in public space and will allow new kinds of information to flow into public spaces, and indeed that is the focus of what we are attempting to explain in this chapter.

2.3   THE IMPORTANCE OF EMBODIMENT

Frith (2012) states that location-based services give the possibility of a 'personal database city' where the subjective experience of spaces is both coded into databases and fed back to users, making the device and location-based service a critical aspect of the subjective experience of space. Embodiment plays a critical role in this, as a means of accessing information in the taken-for-granted processes and behaviours of using mobile devices. We are always embodied in space, and our use of these computational devices is always embodied. While the focus in this chapter is on the effect of LBSN on understanding spaces, without considering embodiment in both location and use of technology such an account would be incomplete.

A very simple opening point for this brief discussion is that different embodied engagements with space can produce different ways of experiencing a space. As Richardson (2007, p. 206) explain: 'every human-technology relation is also a body-tool relationship, and as such every mobile-body merger invokes certain kinds of being-in-the-world, and particular ways of knowing and making that world'. Embodiment can therefore be understood as 'inherently open, allowing us to incorporate technologies and equipment into our perceptual and corporeal organisation' (MacColl and Richardson 2008, p. 104).

> In the context of everyday activities, the experience of one's own corporeal schema is not fixed, but encompasses a range of potential body-aspects and body-images in the form of material and technological mediations, and cultural and historical contexts. (Richardson 2007, p. 206)

To exemplify this, we can borrow Richardson's (2007) example of the act of learning to drive, and the effect this experience has on the body. When an individual learns to drive they have to develop a *mode* of embodiment that goes beyond an understanding of the body that just consider the body alone. In learning to drive, we co-ordinate our feet with different functions of the car, our hands with different functions again, our eyes and head movements with both looking ahead and behind through the reflections of mirrors and our posture to sit behind the steering wheel in a position to make all these extensions of the body to drive the vehicle. Indeed, the car, as a technology-body merger, requires an altered appreciation of distance, position and orientation. Richardson (2007, p. 206) explains: '[within] the material shape and capacities of the car, we adjust our physical deportment, spatial orientation, and our entire physical relationship'. The boundaries between the body and technology are not as delineated as they may seem at first; the body is shaped by the technology, just as the technology (in this case the car) has been shaped itself by the body. This is significant to our argument in this chapter as it opens the suggestion that the physical use of smartphones have the *potential* to produce new embodied understandings of spaces. Just as the car manipulates and disciplines the body in particular ways, the physical practices of use of smartphones and the spaces that smartphones are used in may also combine to produce new, embodied understandings of space.

In approaching the blurring of the boundaries between the body and technology, it would be foolish not to consider Haraway's (1991) cyborg. As Haraway (2004, p. 7) explains, '[a] cyborg is a cybernetic organism, a hybrid of machine and organism, a creature of social reality as well as a creature of fiction' (Haraway 2004, p. 7). Murphie and Potts (2003, p. 116) add that 'the cyborg is a series of real connections between bodies and machines, but it is also a series of metaphors, or new ways of telling stories in order to negotiate culture'. As a result, the unfolding narratives of smartphones, LBSNs and the body are ways in which new understandings of changing spatial understandings might be gleaned. 'The point, argues Haraway, is that identities are neither given nor essential, unchanging blocks characterised by the same attributes across time' (Siapera 2012, p. 175). The many different embodied interactions that we have with technologies in spaces on a daily basis is equally one way in which these identities are continually made and remade. Merleau-Ponty's (1964) notion of the 'corporeal schema' or 'body image' is a conceptualisation of how the body is made and remade in this way. For Richardson (2007, p. 206) the body's apparent capacity to revise itself using media technologies suggests something *more* fundamental about the relationship between media technologies and embodiment:

> Both *as* and *in* context, our embodiment exists as a complex intersection of physicality and biology, material and cultural environment, somatic memory

and habit. Within this relational ontology qua embodiment and technology, the body is a material-semiotic assemblage with constantly shifting boundaries; but also, in my analysis, as quite literally *mediatropic* – disposed both metaphorically and materially towards media technologies.

What is important for our purposes is that embodiment (and the embodied experience of space) can be altered by the incorporation of different 'technologies'. The use of smartphones could have the potential to produce new ways of 'having a body', but more importantly here new ways of *experiencing* the world. We are arguing that LBSNs have the potential to produce new embodied engagements with space, which likewise may open up new social possibilities and the like. A good example of this potential, and how smartphones and LBSNs might be producing different spatial relations to an environment, is the 'mobile massively multiplayer location-based Role-Playing Game (RPG)' Mogi (Joffe 2007).

Active between 2003 and 2006, Mogi involved players navigating 'an actual geographical city – in this case, Tokyo – at the same time as they [navigated] the game space, which [consisted] of a virtual map of the same geographical space' (Richardson and Wilken 2009, p. 30). The play aspect of Mogi required players to collect an array of virtual objects; ranging from simple things like fruits, to more abstract concepts, like 'the idea of morning' (Ibid). Collecting objects led to points, which were then used to rank players. 'The other key feature of the game…[was] that the onscreen map…which [had] a radius of 500 metres…[showed] the icons of other players present in the same geographical space (Licoppe and Inada 2008, p. 166). Mogi highlighted the possibility of a different kind of physical, spatial and social engagement with space. For example, by embedding itself into the everyday activities of those who played it, Mogi quickly led to users developing an implicit understanding of the different players that occupied different environments. This transformed into a more explicit awareness of different territories. As Licoppe and Inada (2008, p. 12) explained, 'because of the publicity and witness ability of location, the frequent occupation of some areas by a player's icon [were] treated by other players as giving him [or her] rights to specific claims about items there' (Licoppe and Inada 2008, p. 12). Just as it could be suggested 'locations…get new meanings through playing' (Sotamaa 2002, p. 43), it could equally be suggested that the incorporation of new media technologies (such as smartphones) have the potential to produce new understandings of space. The physical incorporation of smartphones, alongside new forms of pervasive play, a feature of LBSNs like Foursquare, could be producing new physical, spatial and social understandings of the urban environment as new embodied approaches to space.

At the same time, these embodied approaches and the spatiality they configure suggest the need to reframe traditionally approaches to play, as play has customarily been regarded as being outside of ordinary life and the day-to-day spaces this comprises (Apter 1991; Caillois 2001; Huizinga 1938/1992). As Caillois (1958/2001, p. 6) tersely puts it, '[there] is a place for play'. For Huizinga (1938/1992) this space is famously contained within the 'magic circle'. Theoretically speaking, this notion of the 'magic circle' insists the play of any given game must occur within a spatially and temporally enclosed area, or playground, and is as such detached from 'ordinary' life. As Huizinga (1938/1992, p. 10) suggests, '[play] is distinct from 'ordinary life' both as to locality and duration'. In this vein, when 'a player steps in and out of a game, he or she is crossing the boundary – or frame – that defines the game in time and space' (Salen and Zimmerman 2004, p. 95). The suggestion of a boundary between play and the quotidian is a sentiment markedly made by other game scholars. Caillois 2001, p. 6), for example, likewise suggests, that play is 'a separate occupation, carefully isolated from the rest of life, and generally is engaged in with precise limits of time and place'. In either case, what is echoed is 'the emphasis . . . on the artificiality of games, that they take place in a space and time separate from ordinary life' (Salen and Zimmerman 2004, p. 78). Within the context of the kind of pervasive play detailed previously, where the play of LBSNs seemingly intermingles with the 'ordinary' space of 'real' world environments this idea is significantly challenged. For example, Foursquare's playful side has the potential the transform how users engage with their surroundings in an embodied sense by altering the meaning attached to the objects and spaces that make up their ordinary lives. This confluence of the physical, digital and playful in turn produces the kind of embodied interactions detailed previously.

Embodied interaction is a concept which concentrates on a set of processes that Paul Dourish (2001) describes as 'the creation, manipulation and sharing of meaning through engaged interaction with artefacts' (Dourish 2001). In terms of LBSN, tangible computing (the physical interfacing with computational devices) is allied to social computing (social networking) and location services embedded in the device (smartphone). The activity of using these devices results in the production of an *embodied agent*. This embodied agent is an agent that interacts with the environment through a physical or virtual (i.e. digitally mediated) body. This model is indicative of the approach to embodiment that we take in this chapter. While the study of user experience often implies a focus on the relationship between the user and a particular artefact, this kind of experience-focussed investigation focuses on the needs, emotions and meanings of people's everyday experiences.

The work of Jason Farman (2012) is an excellent example of an approach to understanding the use of locative media where the relationship between user and mobile computational device is understood through the prism of embedded cognition where embodiment and space are co-constitutive. This approach positions mobile computational devices as things that can reconfigure the way that users can embody that space of which they are co-constitutive. Farman's Merleau-Ponty-inflected approach positions the user as an active part of the mediation of the world with the medium or device, as opposed to a technologically determinist approach that would see understanding of the world shaped by the device. We also consider the contribution of the individual as a meaningful in the process of co-creation of space and understanding of the world. Farman's uses the idea of a 'sensory inscribed body' to position digital media as critical in embodiment. The use of mobile media affects the body, but the body also uses digital media – this gives the body a critical role in the effects of mobile media. The body itself is a necessary vehicle for being in the world, and space is always constructed simultaneously with embodiment in that space (2012, p. 18). Most importantly, Farman confirms the line of thinking that mobile technologies are reconfiguring the ways in which users can embody space and locate themselves in digital and virtual spaces simultaneously.

In summary, we are proposing that LBSN's use as an embodied interaction with space will produce new or different understandings of space for users of LBSN. In order to investigate this, we will draw on research conducted with users of the LBSN Foursquare. Foursquare was developed by Dennis Crowley and Naveen Selvadurai in late 2008, before being launched in 2009. Foursquare functioned in three broad ways (its functioning has changed somewhat after a design and interface change in 2014 where check-ins were delegated to a new application called *Swarm*): it allowed users to 'keep up with friends', 'discover what's nearby' and 'save money and unlock rewards' through checking-in to places or marking location (Foursquare 2014). Foursquare functioned as a social application, a locational application and a game application. In social terms, Foursquare used the GPS functionality of smartphones to allow users to 'check in' at a location, and for this information to be then visible to their foursquare friends. Individuals can leave locational suggestions, or 'tips', as they are referred – user-generated advice concerning a specific location, which other users can see – as well as see the tips left by others. Regarding the playful aspect, Foursquare 'gamified' location, awarding points for check-ins and allowing users to become the 'mayor' of a place once a certain number of check-ins has been reached. Mayors could then enjoy 'real' world rewards (in theory) such as special offers and discounts, as well as having the prestige of other Foursquare users seeing their status. In addition, Foursquare awarded badges for different individual check-ins, as well as combinations of check-ins.

To examine how the use of Foursquare has a role in the understanding of space (and in later chapters, temporality and identity), we draw on two original research projects designed to explore the experience of 'the local' amongst Foursquare users. The first project took place between September 2011 and May 2012, using mixed methods including online surveys, face-to-face interviews, Skype interviews and email interviews of 65 users of Foursquare geographically spread across the globe. The second project took place between August and December 2012, with 22 Foursquare users interviewed, all of whom resided in the southeast of Britain. Both research projects involved post-research thematic analysis that consisted of the careful reading of full interview transcriptions, highlighting and coding material that was of interest to the underlining research questions of this book. This chapter investigates the effect of the use of Foursquare on spatial understanding through three movements: first, we explore the extent to which the playful aspect of Foursquare impacts how users comprehend and approach their environment. Second, we examine whether Foursquare affects the places users go, as well as the routes they choose to get there. Third, we investigate the social aspect of Foursquare, and how this might be felt in terms of embodied approaches to one's environment. We conclude this chapter with some reflections on the impact of spatial understandings facilitated through Foursquare and more broadly location-based social media.

2.4   Extraordinary Ordinary Places (and Spaces)

For many of the users we spoke to, especially those in their 20 s and early 30 s, an outcome of Foursquare use was that it made their day-to-day lives and the spaces these lives take place in *feel* more playful. A rigid distinction between play and ordinary life then, as posited by Huizinga's (1938/ 1992) 'magic circle', is immediately contested by our research. The following extract helps establish this point, as Sarah discusses her desire to engage with this side of Foursquare and the fact that this isn't simply borne out of a longing to play the game *per se* but also a yearning to overcome some of the difficulties she faces on a daily basis as an individual diagnosed with Myalgic Encephalomyelitis (M.E.):

> I'm registered disabled with M.E. and I'm mainly housebound. I liked the look of Foursquare, and started using it as a sort of incentive to get out; like a pedometer makes you want to walk more steps, using Foursquare made me want to break my boundaries a bit; try and go out a bit more than what I did…So Foursquare was just an incentive to get out and get mayorships, and to tell friends and family that I'm out, rather than having to ring them and say I'm at such and such a place today, they can instantly see, when I published my check-ins, where I was and that I was getting out. (Sarah)

For Sarah, the playful side of Foursquare isn't understood as being an appendage to her normal life but rather a functioning aspect of her daily life that enables her to become more involved with her surroundings. In turn, the routine spaces that Sarah encounters are simultaneously spaces filled with the possibility of 'play'. The motivation to attain various mayorships through the accumulation of her check-ins symbolises something beyond the 'intrinsic meaning' (Caillois 1958/2001, p. 7) of the game. The impetus to engage with the app exceeds the ludic structure of Foursquare, while still being inextricably connected to it. Put differently, spaces for Sarah coexist with Foursquare and there is blurring of the 'ethereal line' between Sarah's ordinary life and the life of play. For Sarah, and other users of LBSN in this way, the impact Foursquare as a locative game has is not contained within the 'protective *frame*' (Apter 1991, p. 15) of Huizinga's magic circle but instead seeps out into their daily lives and the physical movements these lives involve. Sarah's ability to manage some of the more pressing anxieties surrounding her illness better, such as an often-overwhelming inclination to stay at home, is indicative of the intermingling of these two spaces. This point is further developed:

> I'm so tired and so exhausted all the time with my M.E. I just can't be arsed, you know, I'll save my energy, but then I think, no, I'm nearly the mayor of this place or I'm close to getting one hundred check-ins at that place. Like

my local pub, I recently got my hundredth check-in there; I knew I was getting close and I would think I'll just go for a quick drink. It is so easy to stay at home, but then I think about Foursquare and ousting my fiancé or something. (Sarah)

The play of Foursquare, and the spatiality it configures, encourages Sarah to engage with her world. Both Emily and Mark express similar sentiments:

I have thought maybe more about going for a drink, but thinking I'm too busy, but then thinking actually if I went I'd get more points... because obviously by doing that and going to different places, then you will ultimately get more points, and then I am ultimately still winning. I'm not allowed to play board games with some of my friends because I'm too competitive. (Emily)

I started wanting to go out more, to check-in to places and to get like points and things like that. I think it's made me want to go out a lot more for some reason. (Mark)

What this demonstrates is that Foursquare can alter how some users understand, experience and interact with their environment. When it comes to examining Foursquare as a locative game, play is no longer assigned a particular space abstracted from other spaces but rather all spaces are filled with the possibility of play. As a consequence of this, the play can be engaged with at any time. This is itself significant given Caillois' (1958/2001, p. 6) suggestion that, 'play is essentially a separate occupation, carefully isolated from the rest of life, and generally... engaged in with precise limits of time and place'. What this particular use of Foursquare suggests is the need for an updated understanding of play, one that appreciates the impact LBSN can have on day-to-day lives and the space use takes place in.

This approach, however, should avoid hyperbole as it is easy to infer from the points made previously that all spaces have been transformed by Foursquare's game element. The suggestion that the game aspect of LBSN alone is responsible for rethinking spaces would be a huge overstatement. Indeed, there is far more to the spatial impact of Foursquare than simply the game mechanics that underpin it. Take the mobile social network Dodgeball for instance. Using Humphreys' (2010, 2007) terminology, it would be an exaggeration to say Dodgeball 'parochialized' all of

Manhattan for all users. Instead, a more measured way of examining the impact of this mobile social network on space would be to state for those users who chose to adopt Dodgeball as a tool to coordinate social interactions, a result of this usage was that their surroundings subsequently felt more familiar. Foursquare doesn't instantly transform all spaces into playful sites of locative interaction and exploration, without the user putting in some effort on their part. In order for this to happen, users need to employ Foursquare in a fashion corresponding with the usage detailed in this chapter. In these circumstances, Foursquare can instigate a different relationship with Huizinga's (1992) magic circle, one that effectively softens the supposed border between play and ordinary life.

Our research shows that Foursquare has the potential, and it is this potential that is significant, to disrupt outwardly 'ordinary' environmental understanding allowing for different (in this instance more playful) meanings. It is helpful here to refer back to the conception of spatiality developed previously (see De Certeau 1984; Lefebvre 1991) as it is precisely because of the active character of space that play is itself possible. As de Souza e Silva and Hjorth (2009, p. 604) suggest: 'following Lefebvre, we might conceive spaces not only as social but also as playful, since play is an intrinsic social movement emergent by the relationships between people'. It isn't so much that Foursquare overlays ordinary life, and the spaces this encompasses, with play but rather that it utilises the active character of space to adjust environmental signifiers in such as a way that the possibility of play emerges. As Nieuwdorp (2005, p. 5) succinctly explains: 'what happens in pervasive games is a change in the relationship between an object and it's accepted conventional meaning that has been constructed in a specific cultural discourse'. The 'magic circle' is not only permeable to the 'real' world through LBSN but also becomes more mobile as a result of the boundless potential of digital overlays on physical space.

2.5 Different Games and Different Routes

We can extend these observations from play to examine the places users subsequently frequent, as well as the routes they use to reach these places as a result of their engagement with Foursquare. To this end, the concept of the *flâneur* (Benjamin 1999) as both a subject position and practice is useful in thinking about the spatiality Foursquare configures. Our research demonstrates that LBSN can explicitly alter how users approach and negotiate their environment. This point is made in the following excerpt as Amy discusses her escalating habit of collecting badges and how this custom often leads to her going to areas she otherwise wouldn't:

> We went out of our way to go past Wembley Stadium so I could get a football badge. (Amy)

What is perhaps most noteworthy about this extract is Amy's admission that her and her partner went 'out of' their 'way' to gain this particular badge. In other words, this isn't a space Amy would encounter in her daily life but instead required a certain degree of labour. A similar point is made in the following text, as Paul considers his desire to reach the top of the Foursquare leader board and that this goal led to him and his friends spending a day checking-in to various places they hadn't been to before:

> I remember there was one specific day, where it went mental. We went on a massive walk around the city, checking in at the parks as we walked through them, we would specifically go to places, extra shops, just to check-in. That was a particularly slow day that allowed us to do that, but it was a good laugh. (Paul)

Echoing the *flâneur* (Benjamin 1999), another symptom of Paul's competitiveness is that he and his friends moved through their surroundings following routes that they hadn't used before. For users who employ Foursquare in a similar fashion, the application functions to reveal the numerous spaces and pathways which surround their everyday lives of which they are not necessarily aware. In contrast to the 'paraochializing' effect of Dodgeball (Humphreys 2007, 2010) where potentially unfamiliar environments are transformed into familiar environments, the locative play of Foursquare in this instance functions in the reverse. Familiar environments are revealed to be anything but familiar and instead full of areas yet to be explored. Foursquare facilitates a revealing of space where the old is made new again:

> There was this thing that highlighted things to do in certain places, and there was London, and one day I decided to check-in at all of the top-twenty things to do. So it was like the London Eye and the Houses of Parliament. So I just walked around London checking-in to these places. So that was partly just being a bit obsessed with the game and also just exploring it a bit. (Ryan)

There was one day when we went to town, we went shopping, and literally every shop we went into we checked-in. We checked-in to West Quay, we checked-in to every shop, then we went for food, we went for lunch, and then we went to a bar, checked-in there. It was just constant. Trying to get the points. (Samantha)

The users who engaged with this aspect of Foursquare were for the most part reasonably young. For instance, Paul is 23 years old and Samantha is 24 years old. For many of the older users we spoke to Foursquare as a locative game was regarded as a rather puzzling pastime that they didn't really understand. This point is made in the following extract by John who recently retired and is 65 years old:

I don't understand it. The first time I heard you got points for checking-in at restaurants or, or, coffee bars or something, I was amazed. I mean I laughed out loud when I found you could become the mayor of somewhere. I just cannot get my head around, at all; the game aspect of it. I'd like to, because I'd like to understand why people would do it. I cannot understand why you would, you know, treat it as a game. I'm actually useless at computer games. I've tried and I've tried and I just cannot do them. I haven't got the patience or the understanding. So, that side of things are a total anathema to me. I do get points, and I do get a little chuckle when it says this is the third time you've checked in so you are the mayor. So again, maybe this is something in the future I'll come to understand it. You know, again, it is just something which I don't understand and I never learnt how to use. (John)

The idea of playfully engaging with space in this manner is something John cannot 'get his head around'. It is 'anathema' to him. This observation is implicitly established in his reasoning for not 'understanding' the playful side of Foursquare, being that he 'never learnt to use it'. This is perceived as something someone of his generation would not have learnt to do or has an inclination to learn to do. While it was often the younger users who engaged with this aspect of Foursquare, these users were nonetheless conscious that such usage was in part spurred on by its novelty and was therefore not something they would likely do for a protracted period of time. That is to say, Foursquare as a locative game has a shelf life. As Henry explains:

Well at the beginning, it is because it's a game. You get the points and the badges. So in the beginning I was quite hooked on the game, so I wanted to be the first one of my friends to get the most points, so I was checking in everywhere that I went. I got over that. It was only really the first few months I used it like that. Now I really only check-in to places that are interesting or exciting, or if something exciting is happening like, for example, when I'm going on holiday I'll check-in at the airport and say I'm going to Spain tomorrow, and if I'm on holiday and I'm in a really nice restaurant or a good place then I'll check-in to those places, but I wouldn't just check-in to Starbucks, today, without you here. (Henry)

There was a time when, probably not straight after I joined, but the time when me and a couple of friends, all got heavily into it for a period of about a week or two, and we would check-in everywhere; we would deliberately go to different places to check in, to get the points. We were having a battle for the leader board, but now it's like a casual thing. I'll use it when I want to say something specific about a place, and I use it more as a tool for Facebook and Twitter, rather than in itself. (Paul)

For Samantha, her use of Foursquare as a locative game has reduced because she is no longer a student and owing to this change in life she doesn't go to as many places as she used to:

I'm not a student anymore so I don't go to as many different places, and I'm not going to check-in to work every single day or something like that. When I first started using it there was a lot of competition in our group of friends; who could get the most points, trying to get each other's mayorships and things like that, so that's what made us use it a lot more. (Samantha)

What is important is that in both cases Paul and Samantha's use of Foursquare saw them engaging with their surroundings in a different manner; evading predetermined and already known routes and going to venues and locations they wouldn't have otherwise visited. This kind of spatial practice has parallels with the art of *flânerie*, and the way in which this nomadic figure would move through his locale without a prescribed sense of direction instead engaging with his environment as an aesthetic canvas to poetically explore and create. As demonstrated by Paul and Samantha, Foursquare can affect how some users engage with location producing a spatiality not bound by a specific destination but more open to the rhythmic movements of location-based play.

2.6   BRAGGING, SOCIAL BONDS AND SOCIAL SPACES

For Huizinga (1992, p. 13) play encourages 'the formation of social groups which tend to surround themselves with secrecy...to stress their difference from the common world by disguise or other means'. This provides another way of approaching how Foursquare users employ this LBSN, concerning the attainment of points and especially the acquisition of mayorships. These features not only transform how the city is spatially experienced – at the same time they elicit different and perhaps deeper social bonds with other users. The deepening of social bonds is itself realised within the qualitatively distinct realm of play, through the social exchanges that surround these interactions. So for some users, it isn't just the play of Foursquare that is important but also the social interactions it produces. This point is made in the following extract while Emily discusses the competition that she shares with one particular friend:

> Every now and then I'll get a snarky text, or I'll send one back. He text me yesterday and said he realized you can only be successful at this if you leave the house, so I said what's wrong, and he said well I've been working at home, and I was like well I haven't. (Emily)

In this example, Emily's higher score led to her 'bragging' as well as the exchange of 'snarky' text messages. This kind of bragging was also brought up by several other participants, including Adrian who when asked to outline the benefits of being mayor of Woking Station replied 'it is just about the bragging rights really'.

An 'extra-ordinary' situation of feeling 'apart together' (Huizinga 1992, p. 106) can be identified in users through the status associated with the accumulation of points and mayorships. As Adrian explains, there is no 'real' world benefit *per se* of being the mayor of Woking Station – it certainly doesn't come with any form of monetary gain. However, what it does signify is a certain importance that differentiates him from other users. As Huizinga (1992, p. 107) posits, '[the] "differentness" and secrecy of play are most vividly expressed in "dressing up." Here the "extra-ordinary" nature of play reaches perfection'. This becomes another way of signifying the 'extra-ordinary' quality of the relationship both socially and spatially. This is demonstrated in the following, when

Richard discusses how his desire to visit his favourite café is at the same time rooted in a desire to beat his friend:

> There was this one time when I was sent a message to say I was one day away from the mayorship, so I thought why wait until lunch, why not have breakfast here as well? I'm going to have to beat him (Ben) at this one. So there was one morning where I actively decided to have breakfast at Brewed Awakening, so that has happened. (Richard)

Ben echoes a similar sentiment:

> So there are a few places where it probably does bother me a little bit. So I want to get the mayorship back here [Brewed Awakening], just because I can't let it stand with Richard, but that's a personal thing. (Ben)

In this respect, it would seem the competition Foursquare produces as a game, as well as the social interactions that can follow in the form of bragging, is important to users. Indeed, Dennis details how the rivalry between himself and his wife to be the mayor of their local gym has altered when he goes:

> I was out on a Wednesday, and my wife was out on a Thursday, and she stole it from me on the Wednesday, and I knew if I went Thursday I'd get it back, so I was like, I don't really feel like it because I was out on Wednesday, but I'm going to go anyway, just to get it back. (Dennis)

Foursquare accordingly has an important social component that seeps into the environments that users frequent. This feature of Foursquare is similar to Humphreys' (2007, 2010) observations concerning Dodgeball, in that the familiarity engendered through mayorships, which signifies a different kind of spatial relationship, can at the same time interact with the social associations that are part of the environment and are thus 'characterised by a sense of commonality among acquaintances and neighbours who are involved in interpersonal networks that are located within "communities"' (Lofland 1998, p. 10). Through this kind of play, users become aware of the other users that also frequent that place on a regular basis. As a by-product of rivalries users then go back to these places again and again, strategically modifying both the frequency and time of trips with a view to either keeping or regaining their mayorships. In turn, the spatial practice of

LBSN doesn't only facilitate an understanding of space intermingled with play but equally utilise this play to deepen the social connections that comprises these environments.

2.7   Physical, Digital and Playful Spaces

This chapter began by examining changing scholarly perspectives on spatiality to help establish the potential impact of LBSN such as Foursquare. To briefly reiterate, the movement from questions exploring temporality to those pertaining to spatiality (Elden 2004) is part of an important shift in the comprehension of space which argues space is never simply given nor neutral, but rather co-created through embodied inter-actions and the sociability these entail (De Certeau 1984; Lefebvre 1991). For Lefebvre 1991 this conceptual shift emphasises the 'lived' character of being 'down below' (De Certeau 1984) amid the flows of people and objects that comprise any environment. This is itself markedly different from cartographic and abstracted spaces of maps. To this end, the *flâneur* (Baudelaire 1964; Benjamin 1999), as both a manner of embodiment and a spatial practice helpfully demonstrates the relationship between different approaches to space and different locative experiences. What the art of *flânerie* demonstrates is that urban movements need not always revolve around a specific destination, but can equally include the aesthetic experi-ence of immersing oneself in the flux of the city. In the context of Foursquare, and more broadly location-based social media, this is an important point. LBSN have the potential to transform the meanings attached to day-to-day objects. A significant part of this transformation is rooted in locative play, and its impact on 'ordinary life', which is itself predicated on the notion of an active character of space established pre-viously. Likewise, these spatial experiences similarly involve a combination of flesh and technology (Haraway 1991), which enables an *embodied agent* with the wherewithal to approach space in a manner commensurate with the experiences detailed previously. Not only does Foursquare suggest an updated understanding of play, one that questions the validity of 'magic circles' (Huizinga 1992) and the assumed distinction between play and 'ordinary life' (Apter 1991; Caillois 2001; Huizinga 1992), it also sug-gests the possibility of new approaches to location which are realised through a confluence of physical and digital space.

This chapter explained these spatial possibilities in three ways. First, for many of the users we spoke to, the pervasive play of Foursquare served to motivate them to spend more time interacting with their surroundings rather than simply sitting in front of their laptops. What was significant about this form of engagement was the various ways in which the 'ordinary lives' of these users were infused with a sense of playfulness. In opposition to Huizinga 1992 and his suggested 'magic circle' of play, for these users the locative play of LBSN altered the spaces they occupy on a daily basis. This transformation involved everyday objects and common spaces and places being granted new meanings through the ludic framework of Foursquare. Notably here, an immersion in ordinary space was simultaneously an immersion in the extraordinary space of play. Secondly, Foursquare led many users to frequent places and environments that they either wouldn't usually inhabit or indeed weren't aware of in their everyday lives. For the most part, these changes stemmed from a desire to acquire points, badges and mayorships. Echoing the exploratory footsteps of the *flâneur* then, and in contrast to the 'paraochializing' effect of Dodgeball (Humphreys 2007, 2010), Foursquare effectively enables a revealing of space that highlights the often erroneous belief in the familiarity of supposedly familiar environments. Indeed, for many users a noted outcome of using this LBSN was that it demonstrated how little they actually knew about the spaces that immediately surrounded them, which they had considered 'local'. Finally, this research demonstrated that the locative play of Foursquare can deepen the social ties users experience in conjunction with the 'ordinary space' that comprises their day-to-day lives. While locative play could, on the surface at least, be dismissed as a rather frivolous pastime, for the users we spoke to it was anything but frivolous. In the various reflections explored previously, Foursquare not only allowed these users to establish a more nuanced and personal connection to their surroundings, it also offered the possibility of a deeper sense of sociability through the socio-spatial transformation of locative play in their everyday surroundings.

CHAPTER 3

Time

Abstract LBSNs are often conceptualised as applications that one can use to explore locations and mark one's movements through the check-in function. Importantly, these applications also carry a 'recursive' function, where a historical snapshot of previous check-ins are presented back to users. This offers an opportunity to review one's own check-in history, much like the popular application Timehop does for social networking sites (and indeed for LBSN if sufficiently configured). This chapter considers why some LBSN users elect to both archive and explore their locations. In using LBSN in this way, users are employing applications as 'mediated memory objects' (van Dijck, The body within, Amsterdam, Brill; 2009). Here, we explore the different ways users interact with their stored spatial past. In order to conceptualise this behaviour with temporality, we engage closely with phenomenological theory on the importance of engagement with technology and technicity as a shaping force on the subjective experience of time. Most importantly, we argue that LBSNs are significantly different from older memory-related practices, and exemplify *why* this is important in terms of the understandings of space and place for users that employ LBSN to record and review their movements over time.

Keywords Time · Memory · Mediated memory objects · Technicity · Phenomenology

© The Author(s) 2017
L. Evans, M. Saker, *Location-Based Social Media*,
DOI 10.1007/978-3-319-49472-2_3

3.1   THE DIGITAL MEMORY LANE

The last decade has seen the highly visible movement of computing and computation from the desktop to mobile platforms. The untethering of computation in this manner has been made possible by two aspects of our ubiquitous mobile computational devices: their very computational nature on the one hand, and their ability to connect to the internet on the other. The continual connectivity of mobile devices has facilitated the emergence of the 'mobile web', where services once limited to the desktop become mobile and where the active facets of mobility are also reflected in the services afforded to us as users of mobile devices. One of the most important effects of this is how mobile computation has given rise to new embodied experiences and social connections facilitated by computation, in places where this was previously impossible. The use of smartphones and LBSN applications have allowed for the surfacing of what De Souza e Silva (2006) refers to as 'hybrid space'. This 'hybrid space' occurs when the information and data carried by digital technologies and physical spaces are combined. With the right devices and applications, users can interact with their whereabouts in a manner that moves beyond earlier mobile social networks such as Dodgeball (Humphreys 2010). Space can be understood as constructed through the use of tools (Soja 1996; de Certeau 1984; Heidegger 1962; Lefebvre 1991), and embodiment can be understood as not limited by the body (Richardson 2005; Ihde 1993; Merleau-Ponty 1962). Through allowing its users to engage with public space in a digitally mediated and playful manner, LBSNs have the potential to produce different embodied approaches to space, just as LBSN offer the possibility of extending social connections in new ways (Evans 2015) as our previous chapter has argued.

In the context of time, this shift is significant as the cataloguing of movements over time through the interaction with mobile devices allows for a new mode of reflection upon the intersection of mobility and location and the passing of time. The body of research analysing how locative technologies mediate the relationship between technology use and physical or digital spaces supports the supposition that relationships to physical space have altered through the use of locative media (see Wilken 2008, 2011; Crawford and Goggin 2009; De Souza e Silva and Frith 2010; De Souza e Silva and Sutko 2011; Wilken and Goggin 2012). Research also supports the notion that mobile media itself alters the way that users relate to physical space in a confluence of location and digital networks that mediates geographic places (Campbell and Ling 2009; Gordon et al. 2013;

Martin 2014, p. 180). The ubiquity of connectivity with mobile communications (Okazaki and Mendez 2013), the perpetual contact with social ties and continual potential of accessibility of social ties that creates a continual co-presence (Ling and Horst 2011) and the possibility of instant interactivity with others (Campbell and Kwak 2011) are the features of mobile internet use that create the possibility and affordance of a transformation of the experience of place when using mobile media. Much of the research in this area has concentrated upon the effects of using LBSN on space, in the manner of this body of research and the tone and intent of our previous chapter. However, the temporal dimension or effect of the use of locative media and LBSN has not received the same degree of investigation from researchers. The effects of technology are never merely spatial (in that technology remakes or reveals space anew) as technology also has important effects on the temporal aspect of human experience (Heidegger 1977). While research on the effect of technology on temporality is numerous, the focus is often on the 'speeding up' or acceleratory properties of modern technology (particularly with regard to digital technology, see Lewis 2014; Pasquale 2014; Dormehl 2014). However, with regard to the effect of usage of computational mobile devices on the phenomenological experience of time, research is scant (Saker and Evans 2016b). This chapter addresses this lacuna through an analysis of qualitative data derived from two studies on the LBSN Foursquare.

Our analysis here is linked closely to phenomenological reflections on the relationship between engagement with technology and time. Our aim is to offer an explanation of the effect of LBSN use on the subjective experience of temporality, and we utilise phenomenological theory to do this as this theoretical approach allows us to focus on the subjective experience of time and temporality among users of LBSN. Phenomenology refers to a range of theories that look to understand how the lived-in experience of everyday life is altered by our interaction with tools and technologies. Specifically, we refer to how technicity (the role of technology in everyday life, Bradley and Armand 2006, p. 3) has a critical role in orienting humans to time (Stiegler 1998). Basically, we argue that technology and the use of technology shapes the present as a phenomenological experience. Technology is the element in the world that 'brings-forth' or draws the past in anticipation of the future in its use. Confused? Okay, maybe an example will help. When you load Facebook on your smartphone to find out what is going on at the moment, that present is being shaped both by the past and the projection to the future.

You are drawing on the past both in intention and use of Facebook; you are in a mood that is the character of your intention of use, and this mood is substantially dependent upon your past interactions with the platform. At the same time, Facebook structures the immediate past of your peers in a particular way, through their status updates and ordering this information. This past is drawn forward into the present as you use the app to see what is going on 'now'. While this is happening, the future (i.e. your continuing use of the app or what you are intending to do after using the app) draws a horizon of your actions that limit or contextualise what you are doing in the present. In this sense, Facebook is shaping the present through its use, by bringing the past and future into your experience of the present.

This phenomenological experience of the present is a result of the encounter with an object (and for our purposes the object we are interested in is the internet-enabled smartphone), and that encounter itself has a particular character or mood (Evans 2015). From this, we borrow heavily from the philosophy of Martin Heidegger, who argues that that the temporal experience comes from an orientation to the future that allows the present to emerge. As such the experience of the present as a view into the anticipated future is closely related to Heidegger's ready-to-hand/present-at-hand dichotomy. Heidegger's dichotomy concerns a differentiation between an object (that is present-at-hand) and an object in use (that is ready-to-hand) that is withdrawn from our circumspection while in use. The object being used is projected towards a future in its usage when ready-to-hand. Again, let's reflect on this when using Facebook on your phone. When the phone sits in your pocket not being used (although it is still working away transmitting and receiving data even when there in your pocket, see Kitchin 2014) it would be the present-at-hand (*Vorhandenheit*) state of the device. When the device is taken out of your pocket and used, it is ready-to-hand (*Zuhandenheit*). When in this ready-to-hand state, your attention is drawn not to the device itself but *what you are using it for*; the physical dimensions and properties of the device (weight, size, colour, etc.) withdraw from your attention while the use of Facebook becomes the focus of attention. In this state, we are anticipating a future and drawing on the past to structure the present.

When we adopt this approach to digital media use and time, the now or present is contingent upon what is present in the sense of available or ready-to-hand i.e. the application and device (Stiegler 1998, p. 222). In the case of LBSN, as a particular hybrid of object (the phone) and application we observe a particular manner of orienting the user both in time and towards time. The present is shaped in a particular manner through LBSN use. The focus of this chapter is to understand what this particular orientation or manner to time is with regard to LBSN, through our engagement with user's experiences of LBSN and the manner in which the applications are used.

We have reflected that a key term in this analysis is technicity, and traditionally reflections on technicity with regard to time and temporality are negative: in such analyses time is often seen as being reduced to quantitative measures and because of this time itself is 'annihilated' in a phenomenological, experiential sense. A perfect theoretical example of this comes from Heidegger's reflection on clock time, where time from a clock is never past or future, but only shows the 'now'. This is what Heidegger calls the logic of the 'gigantic' (Heidegger 2012) where the logic of modern technology is to encourage entities (i.e. people) to understand the world in quantitative terms. In this chapter though we don't argue along these lines; instead, we contend that LBSN through their use as a 'mediated memory object' (Van Dijck 2009) co-produce an orientation to time that is far more complex than simple quantification. Again, we can borrow something critical from Heidegger. From *Being and Time*, Heidegger identified that *care* is both the temporal structure of *Dasein* (being-there) that orients present and future activity and the corporeal, affective dispositions that involve the training of gesture and comportment to complete particular tasks. If you like, care is both how we are in terms of using things and how we are in time in terms of understanding time. When we take something into care (in its ready-to-hand usage, such as using Facebook) our use of the thing is both in a particular manner (our gestures and usage) and that usage is orienting us towards time in particular ways. So, when a user of a LBSN uses the application as a mediated memory object, that user is engaging in an activity that takes the application (or object) into care in a particular way, to record and recall events and places as mediated through the functioning of the device (see Evans 2015, pp. 41–50 for a detailed discussion of care with regard to LBSN). Rather than annihilating time, we are looking here to understand how the technicity of LBSN restructures the understanding of time and reflection upon time for the user.

Bernard Stiegler's (1998, p. 174) concept of *epiphylogenesis* (a new stage in evolution in which humans overcome their genetic heritage and develop new ways of being through technological innovation) is useful in considering how one uses LBSN as a memory object. For Stiegler, culture becomes possible itself through the inorganic organisation of memory and the use of LBSN is a way of organising in this manner. In doing this, the LBSN makes a particular culture possible (and therefore the possibility of reflection upon said culture is possible). In performing this exteriorising of oneself technologically (Stiegler 1998, p. 141) through the use of LBSN, there is the possibility of knowing about oneself and the personal narrative of one's life by being able to project oneself from the past into future action. This point can be developed further in light of Wendy Chun's (2011, p. 137) argument that software is always embodied and in being embodied it grounds memory; doing this creates an 'enduring ephemeral' that has the promise of lasting forever. In this case, that 'forever' is temporally bound as the future and so the use of software is always a projection to the future. Jussi Parikka (2012, p. 90) also contributes to this line of thought, arguing that digital memory forces a re-thinking of memory, perception and organisation. In the research discussed in this chapter concrete examples of the use of LBSN to record events and recall memories from users are analysed to illustrate how LSBN (through the ability to record and recall space and time in a particular manner) act to shape the present through both a 'bringing-forth' of past events (temporally and spatially) and projecting the user to the future through the possibility afforded to the user to record and log their movement and temporal location. Due to this, LBSN do not simply annihilate temporality through quantification; these applications inorganically reshape memory as they also reshape temporality and spatiality.

Time itself, and how time is reshaped by technological use, is also something that requires a little reflection at this juncture. On the idea of annihilation of time, Levinas (1987, p. 48) uses the example of insomnia in *Time and the Other* as a phenomena when time and therefore the temporal dimension of our existence (our being-in-the-world) never ceases; it continues onwards with no end point. Levinas characterises such an existence as an annihilation of its own being, with no breakages and end points to allow reflection and consideration of the time one spends existing. The insomniac just 'is', and this 'is' is meaningless. This constant stream of being is anathema to being as it results in a rupture between the individual and other entities in the world, and the ways that we can relate to these other beings in order to orient ourselves to time and temporality. Therefore, the importance of time for our very sense of being human is clear – delineated time allows for events to be clearly defined from one another, and events can be reflected upon and understood. The role of LBSN in its use as a mediated memory object allows for this sort of creation of discreet events in time. Without this kind of discreet event created through our interactions with other people and things in the world, then being becomes one long stream of time, annihilating the meaning of being itself as it continues forth. Here, we want to understand more closely what the nature of the 'time' created by LBSN use is, and how this is created through the practices of use of LBSN.

If the use of Foursquare is primarily to mark physical presence in a place at a particular time, then as we argued in the previous chapter using that check-in to share acquires cultural capital. Checking-in at a place may lead to the acquisition of a mayorship, which may then be employed by certain users as a symbolic way of underlining their connection to the places they most often frequent. Perhaps a user might use a check-in to confirm the authenticity of their relationship to a place, such as frequent check-ins to football grounds. In doing this, check-ins can also become a method or mode of continuing an identity project. In this kind of activity, users may alter the venues that they choose to frequent or check in at according to their own reflexive understanding of themselves. In this sense users are selecting the places they think they should be associated with, and this use of LBSN in identity will be the focus of the next chapter of this book. Users can choose to check-in to places in order to document, in a locational sense, their day-to-day movements. This activity forms a digitally stored archive of the movement s of the user that can be reviewed in the future, shared in the present and planned in the past. This archive becomes a digital record that can is further enhanced with images, text about the event or feelings on the place or simply a timestamp that contextualises the location temporally. LBSN have become a way of remembering spatial engagements as well as their significance. As House and Churchill stated (2008, p. 300), '[a] visible shift in memory in recent years has been the increasing availability, sophistication, capacity and portability of consumer ... capture/record technologies'.

These uses of social media, and LBSN in particular in our case, have been responsible for what Andy Hoskins (2011) refers to as the 'connective turn'. This refers to how 'the formation of memory is increasingly *structured* by digital networks, [with] memory's constituting agency [being] both technological and human' (Van Dijck 2011, p. 402, emphasis added). In using LBSN, the present is restructured by the projection of the event of checking-in into the future. This projection is a structuring of the present as a memory in the future, with the check-in already being positioned intentionally as something that will be recalled as a memory (either by the user or by the application reframing this in the future as a memento of the past) as past check-ins are recalled into our present. This duality of function (calling activities or locations from the past and storing activities for the future) indicates that LBSN are more than a mere modern technology that simply annihilates time. These technologies act as particular memory enabling devices that have their own character thanks to the manner of their functioning. The remainder of this chapter will explore this contention and add nuance to that particular character through an exploration of user experiences.

This chapter again reports on two original research projects designed to explore the spatial and social experience of Foursquare users. As in the previous chapter, the first project was conducted between September 2011 and May 2012, using mixed methods including online surveys, face-to-face interviews, Skype interviews and email interviews of 65 users of Foursquare geographically spread across the globe. The second project took place between August and December 2012, with 22 Foursquare users interviewed, all of whom resided in the southeast of Britain. The post-research thematic analysis for this chapter involved the careful reading of full interview transcriptions, highlighting material that was of interest to the underlining research question regarding how usage affected the experience of time.

3.2   THE RECORDING OF AND REPLAYING OF SPACE AND LOCATION

The basic argument we follow here is that in using Foursquare to record movement, the application acts to store the physical location and act as a memory aid for the user. As such, the application (when ready-to-hand, to use Heidegger's term for an object in use) is both structuring the present (i.e. the activity of checking-in) and projecting towards a future event or space. Spatial movements and the memory of these movements can be documented and structured by Foursquare, a process which is important to Henry owing to his recent move to his new home in London:

> Yeah. So for like the last six months to a year I've used it to, one, keep a track of the places I've been to, especially since I moved to London last year, I like to keep track of pubs I really like or restaurants, so I can say in six months' time, this was that place I went to and liked, so I can go back there. When I

first arrived to London me and some friends did a little pub crawl with some pubs, and I wanted to go to one of those again a couple of weeks ago, so I looked over my history, which took me a few minutes to figure out, and then I found it. (Henry)

Henry uses Foursquare to both keep track of his movements and to review his movements over time in the act of familiarising himself with a new, unfamiliar place. Here, Foursquare acts to structure the present by focussing on the future in one instance and to structure the present in bringing-forth the past in the other. The orientation to time through the use of the application is therefore a function of the manner of use or mood of the user (Evans 2015) rather than a fixed manipulation of temporality through quantification of time. What we can observe is that Henry is not annihilating time or experience; his use of Foursquare is restructuring the manner of his being-at places and acting to serve as a way of self-tracking his movements in the future. This projection to the future is a familiar feature of responses from users across the research.

How did I get in to Foursquare? I can't really remember. I've used it for a long time, because I like to collect data on myself, where I've been or if there is some interesting place that I would like to come back to in the future, so I can check from time to time. That was why I downloaded the app. I want to have the history of my own data; where I have been or what kind of TV programme I've watched. I just like to collect that kind of data on myself. (Robbie)

The curation of a history of personal movements is something found frequently in the use of Foursquare in our research and indicates a very prevalent mode of use of this application and LBSN in general. This use of Foursquare is rooted in a desire to keep track of where the user has been on a daily basis:

Yeah, it's got to the point where, if it is anywhere new that I've been, or somewhere kind of nice, like a nice restaurant, or if I want to even just tweet something related to a place, even though you can tag you location in the tweet, I would do it via Foursquare. I guess, probably yeah, to keep a track of where you've been. When Facebook launched their places, I thought, I don't want to use that, I'll just keep using Foursquare, because I've already got a list of where I've been; I'll keep it all in one place. (Paul)

> Yeah. I do quite like the idea of having a record of what I've done and where I have been, in a kind of diary kind of way, in a digital footprint kind of thing, even though I've never done anything with that, and I'm not even sure how much they store. (Ryan)

These examples are indicative of the kind of usage of LBSN where LBSN affords users the possibility of recording their daily movements. These movements are translated into events, in that they are recorded as where they've been and what they were doing. When Ryan mentions a 'digital footprint' in his response, he's inadvertently illustrating the main principle of the inorganic organisation of memory (Stiegler 1998, p. 178). It is this kind of usage that underpins how the LBSN takes the form of cultural memory object within a culture of creating, storing and curating data on oneself. This activity is indicative of the projecting forwards of one's activity in checking-in to Foursquare; the check-in (present) becomes part of the memory of self as obtained from the application (future, to reflect on the past). This is how LBSN as technologies (through their technicity) structure time – in essence, this is their effect on temporality as a function of their effect of their use in a spatial manner.

3.3   AUTO-RECALL: THE RECALL OF LOCATION THROUGH LBSN

As we've already heavily alluded to in this chapter, one of the key ways that LBSN affect temporality is through their curative function. What we are referring to is how these applications may refer the user back to their past check-ins or locations. This could be through a reminder as someone tries to check-in or access location-specific information in a place – 'you were here on . . . ' – or through a periodic reminder of when people were in specific locations (the third-party application Timehop is a particularly popular example of this service). The Foursquare application also acts to facilitate this curation by alert users to their past movements. This activity takes the form of an email generated by the application to give reminders of where the user was in the past, on that day:

> There's also a weekly email from Foursquare that just lists everywhere you were a year ago that day. You look through that and more often than not it's the office, the train station, home sort of thing, but then occasionally you'll

be on holiday and you'll go, I remember being there. It just jogs your memory. You wouldn't think that was a year ago. (Dennis)

Dennis specifies the way that locational past returns to him, detailing 'everywhere' he was 'a year ago that day'. The generation of the email is automatic; Foursquare applies an algorithm to collect all check-ins from the date in the past years of usage, and pushes this information out to the user that has elected to receive these communications. As Dennis states, most of the information is mundane and not of any interest but the occasional update acts as a memory aide to specific events, drawing the past into the present and allowing for both reflection and a realisation of the journaling of one's movements and location that is a part of the use of LBSN.

Like I said earlier, about having an email every day that tells me where I was last year, and that's interesting. I saw that yesterday, last year, I was going back to school, so that was interesting to see. (Mark)

For Mark, the email acts in an interesting way to lead to a rediscovering of the places he was in last year. In informing users of specific events, the LBSN helps form a narrative account of the past that is co-constitutive of memory and indicates the application's status as a 'mediating memory object'. What we mean here is that the memory Mark has is co-constructed with the application; his check-in forms part of that memory. The memory is jogged by the information in the email, but the activity at the time involved that check-in and use of LBSN, and so the use of the application and the activity of the application in the future both are contributory factors in this memory – hence its co-constructed nature. In a similar comment, what is important to Amy about receiving this information from Foursquare is that it 'transports' her 'back there'. In this sense, the information provided helps her to reconnect to her locational past:

Because it will do your tweets and I think your Facebook status as well. I think it does all of them now. But I love that, seeing what you did a year ago. Like this morning I found out this time last year I was shopping for carpet, and there was just a whole list of carpet shops, and it just suddenly does, it just does transport you back there, and you think, God I remember that. (Amy)

The use of LBSN as a tool for recording day-to-day spatial movements clearly does have an effect on how users engage with their locational history. In these examples the locational past can be seen as permeating into the present. These reminders act as an aid to memory that prompts a remembering in the user of what they were doing on particular days in previous years. Accordingly, we can argue here that this facility provides the user with a different kind of locational experience. This experience is one where the past, locational speaking, is brought forth into the present and in doing so structures the present in a particular way. Foursquare in these instances acts as an aid to memory that has the effect of deepening connections to the places that users frequented in the past and recorded using LBSN. At the same time this use of LBSN also illustrates *how* LBSN differ from other memory-related practices, such as keeping a diary (in a written form) or taking and collecting photographs (non-digitally). The digital information stored by the application is easily configured and pushed to users in order to provide information on the past. This does not exclude the possibility that users can go through older memory-related pastimes on a daily basis and then uncover where they were on such and such a day. However, that would be a laborious task in comparison to the way LBSNs operate in an automatic manner without input or conscious effort or circumspection of the user. Foursquare in these instances makes this practice far easier. For the users that employ Foursquare as a mediated memory object, they do not have to search for their spatial past. Their spatial past finds them automatically thanks to the pushed information that derives from the data that these users contributed to the databases of the application as a result if their check-in. The result of this activity is that 'the boundaries between present and past are no longer given' (Van Dijck 2011, p. 404), but rather constructed along location-based lines.

As a consequence of how Foursquare and other LBSN restructure temporality and the kind of past spatial connections Foursquare allows, for some users the accuracy of their check-ins are important.

> Most of my check-in history is to see when and what I've done. If I'm sat in my office and I've checked-in to every other office around me, I'm going to look back at that in a year and go, well I wasn't in these offices what's going on? (Dennis)

The essential criteria for the Dennis in using Foursquare as a mediated memory object is the authenticity of the locational information documented. Dennis is attempting to keep a truthful, accurate account of where he's been on a day-to-day basis for the purpose of reviewing this in the future. Dennis' ultimate aim (and his motivation for his use of the application) is to be able to look back at activity in the future and reclaim locational memories that did 'happen' rather than being perplexed by erroneous spatial information that didn't occur. As this is Dennis' intentional purpose of using Foursquare, he desires 'real' check-ins. His use of Foursquare does more than simply record significant locational experiences because of this intentionality. Instead of idly using the application, Dennis is deliberately archiving all spatial movements on a day-to-day basis as and when they occur. The recording of both the significant and the banal is an important aspect in his authentic, co-created memory of location. When we argue that Foursquare can function as a technological form of spatial memory, Dennis is an exemplar of this activity but he is far from alone in using LBSN in this way.

> Yeah, it's just nice to keep a record. I think it is easy. I noticed the other day, when I was looking through it, when I knew I was coming, and I was like I remember when we checked-in there that day. It's kind of like a memory lane; a digital memory lane almost, related to places you've been. (Paul)

From Paul's perspective, his Foursquare use is tantamount to the construction of a 'digital memory lane' for the places that he's been to in the past. This is an important metaphor (as we alluded to previously), as it works to emphasise that the use of Foursquare as a tool for locational memory while also emphasising the aspect of day-to-day movements as and when they occur with a view to attaining a form of spatial preservation. This kind of use and understanding resonates with Doug, an avid AFC Wimbledon fan (a supported-owned football club based in South-West London that play in the third tier of English and Welsh professional football):

> I'm an AFC Wimbledon fan, and so I have travelled to a lot of away games, going to these weird grounds in the middle of nowhere, and I was reading a book recently talking about some of the games, and I did not have any recollection of being at certain games, and as I was reading it I was thinking I wished I'd gone to that. It was only when I spoke to my dad, who seems to have a better memory than me, he'd say you did go, and then I'd do a Google search and find I'd written stuff about the match online. There was

one when I'd done a whole report about being somewhere that I didn't even know. So I sort of see Foursquare as a way of recovering these lost moments. Some people may remember every moment of every game they go to, but I don't; I don't see the need necessarily. But when you forget entire chunks of being somewhere else, that's not good. (Doug)

Doug not only records his location with the application but also acknowledges that the application acts as a mnemonic device in recalling events and locations that he cannot consciously recall without this memory aid. Indeed, Doug uses an entire digital media infrastructure as a method of recalling when he was at matches and where those matches were with his Foursquare check-ins playing a role alongside his blogging or match reports. For someone that attends many matches in many places there is the impression here that they can meld into one, or the different events cannot be differentiated. Recalling Levinas earlier in this chapter, the making discreet of each location by the LBSN provides an authenticity and character to each place that is dependent upon the check-in, the storage and the pushing and retrieval of this information in the future. What these examples are intended to demonstrate is that for some users, Foursquare is employed as a 'mediated memory object' (Van Dijck 2009). As Van Dijck (2009, p. 168) explains, 'memory is not simply triggered by objects, but happens *through* these objects'. For these users it is through their use of Foursquare that their spatial past is both stored and can subsequently be recalled. For 'Doug', this is important as he notably explains it allows him to recover experiences that would have otherwise been either forgotten or 'lost'.

These examples also illustrate that for some Foursquare users, the application is seen as being a secure and reliable way of preserving their day-to-day spatial movements. What we mean here is that this application is perceived as more secure than older, non-digital memory-related pastimes, because of the way that LBSN store, structure and provide data for users. That said, whether Foursquare is in actuality a better or more secure means of preserving the past is not what is necessarily important. What is important is that for some users the use of LBSN feels more secure and enduring. This is where the significance of the use of LBSN lies as it allows individual to reconnect to the places they once inhabited in new and 'interesting' ways. Hoskins' (2011) suggestion of a 'connective turn' offers a viable way of approaching how memory may be changing as a result of its nascent structuring within digital networks. In these examples, the 'connective turn' is exemplified in how users intentionally record their location as a habitual behaviour that is projected forwards as an intentional memory in the future. The memory is therefore always co-constructed – memory is not dependent upon LBSN, but these kind of memories of location are facilitated by and include LBSN use as a fundamental part of their affective and recalled dimensions.

3.4   THE LOCATIONAL PAST AND ITS PRESENT POTENTIAL

It has been argued that 'new media' technologies, such as smartphones and Foursquare, enable the 'self' to be drawn-out or illuminated in innovative and interesting ways (Tian and Belk 2005). As Hoskins (2011, p. 26) explains, '[smart phones] and other highly portable devices act as prosthetic nodes that extend the self across an array of communication and consumptions networks, personal and public'. We noted in our analysis that LBSNs are employed by some users as a way of 'extending' themselves spatially and temporally, through the meanings attached to the place or location that they have committed to digital memory through a check-in. This point is to some extent borne out in the examples we have already detailed in this chapter. There is additional significant though in the way in which Foursquare records the past, and this comes from the digital manner of the application. What we have noted is that this digital way of doing things adds a different character to the way that users conceptualise and approach their spatial pasts and locational memories. The availability of a digital tool for creating a memory bank of movement and location is in itself something that can prompt, entice and motivate users to engage with applications. This sense of possibility is demonstrated here as 'Jane' discusses her plan to visualise her travels, using the similar-to-Foursquare (but now defunct) LBSN Gowalla:

So I'd stopped using it [Gowalla] by the time Facebook had bought it, and I switched to Foursquare. So the reason that happened, I guess, it was actually the very start of this year that I stopped using Gowalla and switched to Foursquare, and the reason actually was because I didn't know anyone on Gowalla, because it was primarily used in Norway, where I don't really have many friends, and I had been using it, Gowalla, almost as a diary to keep a track of where I'd been, especially as when I first got it in 2010 I was doing loads of travelling and conferences and stuff like that, and I was thinking this is cool, I get to go to all these cities and all these countries, if I check in to each one, I can't remember what the Gowalla term is, then I'll get a little map sort of a thing, and there were various tools where you could export your Gowalla stuff, if you put in your user name and password, to a visualisation, and I thought this is really neat, I'm going to make a 2010 map or a 2011 map, and then do that. (Jane)

LBSN use offered Jane the possibility of aggregating and visualising her spatial movements and locations, and this positions the application as a mnemonic geographic information system (GIS). The possibility of a visualisation that helps the user understand their locational past through a transformation of check-in information into a new media form with its own curative practices and possibilities for use is also commented upon by David:

Well they have this really cool visualisation where they link this app that is a big map of the world and you see all your check-ins as dots with lines coming out of them; it maps your whole journey. (David)

It is noteworthy that both users are engaged in occupations that revolve around data, which may be critical in why they may choose to employ LBSN in this manner. These users have data-intensive occupations and when we are looking to why they might be interested in the potential for new way of recording the self through the technology, this comfort with and acceptance of data in everyday life could be an important indicator of why these users have conceptualised and normalised the use of LBSN in this way. For Jane and David, the digital preservation employed by the likes of Gowalla and Foursquare means that their archived memories have the potential to be restructured and consumed in ways that are not possible when using other mediated memory objects. At very least, it would be extremely difficult to achieve the kind of visualisations that these users want if they were attempting to do this with, say, written diaries. Take Jane's desire to present her 2010 and 2011 travels digitally. This is a strategy that would have provided her with a markedly different mode of conceptualising and recalling her locational past than if she was to use a non-digital method.

So, what is important to some users such as Jane and David is that LBSN like Foursquare and Gowalla provide them with access to an accumulated locational past. This stands in opposition to fragments of information that are characteristic of older memory-related practices. When adopting the kind of technique of memory encoding and preservation that these users employ, the past becomes in its preserved state a '*residual abundance*' (Virilio 1997, p. 24). This means that the past becomes figuratively comparable to a camera raw image file, open to many pathways of exploration, much like the Arcades to the *flâneur* (White 2008; Benjamin 1999; Gleber 1999; Shields 1994; Tester 1994). Robbie touches on a similar point as he discusses designers and their obsession with visualising data:

> I think I like it. I don't know, because I am a designer, I think a lot of designers are obsessed with data visualisations. There was this one designer and he tried to make an algorithm of himself [laughs]. So it has got all of the lines, and graphs, with data visualisation of where he has been during the last year, of how many beers he has drank, with the top three places he has been. So that kind of thing. (Robbie)

What these examples of Foursquare use emphasise is that there is a perceived significance about LBSN like Foursquare in their ability to record the spatial past in a fashion that can then be approached in fresh and interesting ways. This is a result of the digital means of storage of data, which through application programming interfaces (API) provision allows for software designers and other parties to design complimentary applications that can allow the memory of location to be remediated into new forms. While discussing the reasons he thinks he uses Foursquare, Doug details another way his locational past could be utilised:

> Well I think I've figured it out; I figured it out for myself when I last went on holiday. Let me give you my answer, because I was like I'm not sure why I'm using this. Initially it was research. My wife is not into social networking at all, Facebook or Twitter, whereas I check in to what beers I'm drinking, what locations I go to, tweet this that and the other, and she doesn't know half of it because she isn't on half of the networks. People often say your wife must know everything you are up to, and I'm like no because she doesn't use any of this stuff. Not that any of it is private. So she's always like what are you doing, why are you checking-in here and whatever, and I'd say it's quite fun you know. So I was trying to think about it, and lots of people would say why do you bother, because it seems quite pointless – on face value it does seems quite pointless – and then we went on holiday and we were checking-in at places; now I'm not very sentimental, but she is, so we went back, and we tried to stay in the place she went as a kid, and we took our kids, and we

went to a lot of locations she had been to, and she had the whole lot, a photo album, and what we tried to do was find those places again and take up-to-date photos of the same locations, and at the same time I'm checking-into these various locations, and then it sort of dawned on me that if this data is public and my ancestors can see it, that same experience could be revisited by me fifty years later, or my family, fifty years later, with reference to the exact moments I was in those locations. I then started to think it is more about looking back; it isn't the checking-in process. (Doug)

At this point we can refer back to Wendy Chun's (2011, p. 137) argument that software is always embodied, and in being embodied software grounds memory. The embodiment of the software (or application if you like) in this case is in the physical location of the user, which is coupled with an affective dimension that relates to the specific event being chronicled. Here, the action clearly is intended to create an 'enduring ephemeral' with the promise of lasting forever. This is what Chun argues is the seductive aspect of digital storage. Doug's understanding of Foursquare and his motives and intentions for using it revolve around how his locational past could be re-experienced at a later date. Foursquare is a way of appeasing his fear of losing 'entire chunks' of his life. Doug isn't simply preserving his day-to-day movements for himself; he is also doing this with the intention of preserving his movements and locations for future generations to come, so that they can vicariously experience his locational past. Some might think this wildly narcissistic but that would be a deeply unfair judgement and would overlook Doug's acute understanding of what it is that LBSN and social media in general do. Doug is aware that this data is stored, that it can be retrieved and that all things being equal it can be retrieved in the future. This is inclusive of all social media, not just Doug's own beloved Foursquare. Whether consciously or not, all social media users are engaging in this kind of preparatory activity for the recalling of their pasts by either themselves or others. So, for some users Foursquare is seen as being a secure way of preserving their past, under-lined by Doug's suggestion that his past could be re-visited in 'fifty years'. A consequence of this desire for personal preservation is Doug's attention to the precise details of location that Foursquare archives:

Now if I check in to somewhere I've checked-in to before, I'm interested in the exact details, like how long ago was it that I last checked-in, what photos did I take of that moment. (Doug)

This kind of granularity and detail in the information stored by the application shapes both the interaction of the user with that information, and the intentionality of the user in the present to store information for this kind of examination in the future. Robbie too exhibits an interest in the level of information that Foursquare can document and store:

> I don't know. I don't know how I got that obsessed. I wanted to know when I had been to certain places; when was the last time. I like to take photos, so I like to keep data on the photos, the date and the location. I'm always keeping track of time. (Robbie)

This indicates that precision with which Foursquare can record the locational past is a critical factor in the use of the application for Robbie (and indeed the other users in this section). These users exhibit a desire to spatially document their movements and Foursquare's potential isn't only rooted in the forging of an accumulative past that can then be visualised in a number of different ways. The potential is also realised in how this or that experience may be shared with others on a durational plane, permitting '[the] very distant past [to be] projected into the present and the future' (Urry 2002, p. 116). In this sense, the locational past isn't simply preserved in one form, but is at the same time open to being relived through various simulations. In other words, Foursquare '[represent] a convergence of past experiences, current life, and future possibilities' (Raine et al. 2012, p. 285).

So, in these cases it is clear that the application acts not as a technology that annihilates time in a phenomenological sense through quantification, but as an object that restructures the experience of time for users that are consciously directed towards using the application in this manner (Evans 2015, p. 44). The significance of LBSNs as mediated memory objects is in the way that they allow users to record details of their life that could be re-experienced at a later date. As Doug puts it, this is the 'fun' of using the applications. Even when Doug is fully aware that others are not able to quantify the value of his activity, and that frequent usage of the service is a potential (or actual) privacy risk, the use of the application as a mnemonic object for future, personal recall of situated, locational events is worthwhile.

With Foursquare's capacity to record daily events spatially, it should not be too unexpected that we found that the application may be employed to provide alternative ways of exploring locations. Some of our Foursquare users reported that the process of engaging with locational information *feels* authentic owing to its user-generated status. These users check-in as a means of gaining personalised locational suggestions and these suggestions are algorithmically pushed to the user from the check-ins of other users. These algorithms assess the check-in histories of a user and the check-ins of other users in that locale to assess the most suitable suggestions and push these to the user through the Foursquare interface. For Doug, the use of Foursquare to chart his own locational history sits in tandem with a desire for Foursquare to 'get better' at applying the movements of his past to the movements of his future, as he explains:

> I'm kind of hoping that the 'explore' feature will get better as it looks at my history for me, and then starts to give me better and better recommendations. I don't want it to be too much at the forefront because it can narrow you. There are lots of studies that talk about how it narrows your field of vision. So I don't want it too much in my face, but if I go to a few places and somewhere similar clicks, because of the data they have collected, it would be good to see a little more of that. So I would probably like Foursquare to use my history more than me. When I review it is more that I need to recall something: did I do this or whatever. Maybe I *am* being sentimental and when I look at this in twenty-year's time I won't be bothered. (Doug)

What we observe here is how the accumulated spatial past of the user is 'folded' back into Foursquare and how the application then frames this data transformed into information in a kind of 'present potentiality' in the form of locational suggestions. This is meaningful here as it illustrates how the application acts to shape the present by framing the future present as a kind of idealised temporal domain where past activity refines the future possibilities of action. This is rather complex: the temporal activity we describe here involves a shaping of past, present and future as an affordance of the way that the application acts as a memory object. The complexity is again beyond the mere quantification of time, as such a complex reorganising of temporality and memory involves a strong affective domain where contextual information marks particular events as significant. As Amy observes, this makes Foursquare feel like an 'organism':

> It is almost like an organism, it learns from what you do, you know, if you use the top picks, it will always come up with the nearest Starbucks; always, whether I like it or not [laughs]. (Amy)

The use of Foursquare to preserve ones locational past allows users to have an 'augmented' relationship with their locational present. The bespoke locational suggestions that users receive when they open their LBSN are rooted in their past movements, locations and check-ins. Users who employ Foursquare in a directed, intentional manner where the use of the application is for specific, life reviewing or life-logging ends feel that the locational recommendations Foursquare provides are in some way more valid or authentic than what they would receive from other less personalised services, such as a guide book. The recommendations from Foursquare stem from their accumulated check-in history, which is the result of their own intentional desire to mark their location and as such is personalised in a way that a traditional media source cannot offer. It is precisely this feature that is significant for Martin, as Foursquare for him is a personalised service ostensibly rooted in his locational 'memories'.

> Admittedly, I'm one of those people who probably over-shares thinking someone cares about it. Like I said before, I use most social media for my own sake. I know I'm just some guy, and I'm probably quite dull, but I like to keep a memory of my life backed up somewhere. Plus, you never know who might get curious. Perhaps I'm relying on my dull nature to prevent someone malicious from stalking me? (Martin).

Martin's self-reflection frames his own check-in activity on Foursquare (and other services) as a means to review his own life history through an externalisation of these experiences as memories to digital services. The acknowledgement of the 'backing up' of this history in digital databanks recalls again Chun's (2011, p. 137) notion of the perception of an enduring ephemeral nature of these services. At the same time, this kind of reflection recalls Stiegler's (1998, p. 174) concept of *epiphylogenesis* as a mode of existence dependent upon the inorganic organisation of memory. Social media data-streams are a way of organising experience into digital memories in this manner. As people exteriorise themselves technologically (Stiegler 1998, p. 141), there is the possibility of knowing their own being by being able to project oneself from the past into future action. There is also the opportunity to review one's own history to reshape the present, and accordingly project oneself into the future based on this now mediated past. All of this activity is contingent upon the permanence of databanks and the validity and integrity of their data. This is also contingent in the present (that is, in the action of the check-in) on the orientation of the user towards a desire or intention to preserve the moment. Additionally, there is a desire to use the information stored on spatial and locational pasts in the future as part of the narrative construction and history of one's life. This kind of usage and the possibility of this kind of usage that Foursquare affords as a mediated memory object are both technologically and intentionally contingent. The mechanisms and operations of software and code are critical in both the possibility and actuality of this externalisation of memory, projection of activity and externalisation of the self through digital means – but so is the intention to apply the application to this end.

3.5 'TIME WAITS FOR NO LBSN...'

This chapter has explored how LBSNs function as a form of technological memory, with the locational past of users that is encoded through their activity on these platforms permeating the present on a daily basis. This present then works to draw attention to and structure the future of the user. This technicity of LBSN is far from limited to the location-based social platforms alone; the temporal structuring of the present through a convergence of past and present is not only confined to those of us that regularly thumb through their volumes of Heidegger's *Being and Time*, but also is a pertinent feature of the lives of anyone that regularly uses major social networking platforms such as Facebook and Twitter. We used Facebook as an illustration of the conceptualisation of time that we use here to describe the temporal effects of LBSN use earlier in this chapter. While LBSN were certainly not the first internet-based platform that exhibited this kind of effect, it is interesting to note that there is clearly a 'social network effect' in LBSN (as befits their name, one might think). Social media with the features of timelines, celebration of anniversaries or past dates and automated retrieval of these events would structure time in this way, as does the reviewing of past posts/check-ins from your own activity or other users. LBSN are therefore fairly regular social networks in this sense. Of course, we have also seen that Twitter and especially Facebook have integrated locational aspects into their own platforms too. In par icular, the check-in service on Facebook (or Facebook Places as it was once known in the dim past of social media, or five years ago for another perspective) mirrors much of the check-in experience of the more common LBSN such as Foursquare and Gowalla. Here again, we see the impact of LBSN on other media and the traces of dead LBSN (as well as living LBSN) in the monolithic social media services that are so commonly used in the average, everyday existence of many digitally enabled people. LBSNs also work to preserves the past in a manner that feels 'secure and enduring' according to the reports of users. Given the demise of many LBSN services though, this contention is itself somewhat troubling. As we noted more than once in the course of this chapter, a belief in Chun's (2011) enduring ephemeral is continually apparent in the discourses of these LBSN users. However, ask a Gowalla user about the permanence of data; following the purchase of the service by Facebook that data disappeared into Facebook's labyrinthine data banks to inform and refine their spatial algorithms and data services, and to be used in their commercial activities. This points to one of the more troubling aspects of the dying out of LBSN platforms and applications: what happens to these spatial pasts? One could look at this in two ways of being concerned. There is the question of data, in that what becomes of it, where and who it is sold to and where is it stored or where does it reside are key questions (particularly regarding security and privacy). On the other hand, there is a humanistic aspect to this in that if users are trying to preserve and curate a spatial past using this technology, what is the effect of losing this service? This may appear a quintessentially 'first world problem' but it does highlight the potentially disruptive consequences of the end of digital platforms and services. From a keen sense of space and time, one might be left with a radically reduced sense of space and hence time if one was to be so inclined to use these services in such a directed manner. Of course, you'll probably live; nothing too fatal about an LBSN going under. Given the hysterical reactions to minute changes in Facebook's user interface over the years it might not be a significant issue, but more than a minor inconvenience in user's lives.

From the material that we have covered in this chapter, it is clear that the spatial past can be approached in various ways, which we summarise as significant for three reasons. Firstly, gathered memories can be considered accumulatively, as a '*residual abundance*' (Virilio 1997, p. 24), through various applications, enabling users to effectively visualise periods of their own past. Secondly, the past in its collective and spatially detailed form has the potential to be shared with others, and thus re-enacted at a later date. This potential is a significant aspect of curating personal locational and temporal histories using LBSN, more so than the reality of these re-enactments taking place. Thirdly, the spatial past is algorithmically remediated by LSBNs and third party applications like Timehop as a means of then delivering personalised locational information. For some users this provides locational suggestions that feel more pertinent, personalised and authentic than those from a guidebook or other media, an example of William Merrin's (2014) me-dia. In this chapter we see the directed, intentional use of Foursquare as a mnemonic or mediated memory object – through an intentional turn to using the application to log one's own location over time – inorganically organising these 'memories' or data along the logic dictated by the code and algorithms of Foursquare.

This remediation does work in the temporal dimension by impinging on the phenomenological present to shape that present and the future intentions of the user. As such, Foursquare – in a particular mode or usage – reshapes past, present and future as a complex digital technology object. Casual use of the game aspect (see Evans 2015, pp. 117–121) of Foursquare or its use as a recommendations service (Evans 2015, pp. 149–150) for businesses and locations would lack the depth of engagement with the application and the practice of both logging information and reviewing the past that identifies the use of Foursquare as a memory object. However, LBSNs (like other social media) still collects these casual interactions in the same way that it collects the serious, and these could be re-appropriated in the form of location-based suggestions to users that could be used to shape the present or now for the user this is pushed to by the application. The design, digital infrastructure and functions of LBSN combine to create a platform that is geared to usage as a memory object – but the intentionality and directed mood (Evans 2015, p. 120) of the user towards the application is needed to realise this temporal dimension. We see this as a feature of other, common social networks, which have been achieving the same for longer but without location as an aspect of their regurgitation of the status update. Except, of course, they also do this now too, thanks to their integration of locational services as a given on their platforms. The complex but pervasive structuring of temporal experience done by LBSN, linked intimately with location, place and the spatial dimension, is a common feature of the leviathans of social media as well as dead or lonely LBSN.

CHAPTER 4

Identity

Abstract Building on the spatial and temporal elements of LBSNs developed in the previous two chapters, the focus here is LBSN use in the context of identity. Specifically, the chapter explores the various ways presenting and archiving spatial movements through LBSN can be called upon to present a certain self to others. Research in this field has indicated that 'self-presentation has moved from examining interpersonal interactions to displays through mass media' (Mendelson and Papacharissi, The networked self: Identity, community and culture on social network sites, London, Routledge; 2010, p. 252), with SNSs offering new ways for people to present themselves to others and '*keep a particular narrative going*' (Giddens, Modernity and self-identity: Self and society in the late modern age, Stanford, Stanford University Press; 1991, p. 54). Drawing on the work of Goffman, The presentation of self in everyday life, Garden City, Doubleday (1959) and his suggestion that identity is the consequence of 'front stage' and 'back stage' behaviours, our analysis extends these insights to LBSN. This understanding is then further developed with reference to Schwartz and Halegoua's New Media & Society, doi: 10.1177/1461444814531364 (2014, p. 1) 'spatial self', which serves as 'a theoretical framework encapsulating the process of online self-presentation based on the display of offline physical activities'.

Keywords Identity · Spatial self · Narrative · Presentation of the self · Self-image

© The Author(s) 2017   63
L. Evans, M. Saker, *Location-Based Social Media*,
DOI 10.1007/978-3-319-49472-2_4

4.1   SOCIAL NETWORKING SITES: SPACE, PLACE AND IDENTITY

As we have suggested throughout this book, to suggest that social media is a big deal does not really do it justice. Social media usage is exponentially growing. Let's take a look at the numbers. In January 2016, there were 2.3 billion active social media users out of a total global population of 7.3 billion. This figure is up 10% on last year's tally (We Are Social 2016). As a consequence of this growth, social media has continued to be a hugely important global medium of communication; a medium that not only impacts the social realm, but equally influences the cultural, political and the economic spheres of many societies today. Broadly speaking, social media refers to various types of online communication platforms. These platforms comprise forums, blogs, microblogs, wikis, social curation sites and Social Networking Sites (SNS). The biggest category of social media is SNS, with prominent examples including Facebook, Twitter, LinkedIn, Google +, YouTube and Instagram, to name but a few. To put things into perspective, as of the first quarter of 2016 Facebook had 1.65 billion monthly active users (Statista 2016), while Twitter had amassed 310 million users, and LinkedIn had accumulated 433 million users. You would be forgiven at this stage for assuming it is only really young people who engage with SNS to post, pin and, on rare occasion, poke. You would be excused for making this assumption, but you would be wrong. 'Use of social media has surged in recent years, initially spurred by young people but now used by all demographic groups of the global population' (Ellison 2013, p. 3). Indeed, millions of people throughout the world interact with SNS on a daily basis, and for a growing number of reasons.

SNS primarily enable 'a culture of remote connectivity for . . . maintaining a variety of social ties to primary and secondary groups of contact' (Mendelson and Papacharissi 2010, p. 251). As a result of this and owing to the growing popularity of SNS, a diverse multi-disciplinary body of research has developed around this field (see Albarran 2013; boyd 2014; Bradburne 2007; Dasgupta 2013; Edwards 2015; Flynn 2012; Issa et al. 2015; Kelsey 2010; Li 2013; Light 2014; Lipschultz 2014; Mallia 2013; Mandiberg 2012; Obee 2012; Partridge 2011; Pătruț et al. 2014; Ryan 2011; Fuchs 2014; Wilde 2012). Research has explored the impact of SNS on education (Dasgupta 2013; Issa et al. 2015), with schools utilising prominent platforms to enhance the teaching experience of their students (Mallia 2013). SNS have been examined within the context of the law (Lipschultz 2014) and politics (Pătruț and Pătruț 2014) with new policies being implemented to police the 'Facebook age' (Fuchs 2014). Research has also investigated the pivotal part social media now plays in business (Flynn 2012) with SNS like Facebook and Twitter becoming integral to many advertising and marketing campaigns (Li 2013; Wilde 2012). Likewise, the communal impact of SNS and their connective potential have been scrutinised with research probing how young people (Edwards 2015) and teenagers utilise social media (Livingston 2008; Obee 2012) to facilitate their 'complicated' social lives (boyd 2014). Alongside this, and importantly for our purposes in this chapter, '[studies] concerning practices of self-presentation and impression management on popular social networking sites ... have increased significantly' (Schwartz and Halegoua 2014, p. 3; Milani et al. 2014; Ellison 2013; Senft 2012; boyd and Ellison 2007; Donath and boyd 2004). It is now widely accepted that people use SNS to 'present a highly curated version of themselves' (Schwartz and Halegoua 2014, p. 3; Mendelson and Papacharissi 2010), enabling 'the possibility for more controlled and more imaginative performances of identity online' (Papacharissi 2011, p. 307). This idea of personal identity being a 'highly curated' process, involving some degree of choice, suggests something important about the relationship between SNS and identity itself that warrants further attention.

The proposition that identity is something people actively work on has its roots in late modernity, when the ontological anchor (that identity is in some way fixed) restraining the concept of identity began to loosen (Beck and Beck-Gernsheim 2002; Turkle 1996; Giddens 1991; Lash and Friedman 1992; Butler 1990). The work of Giddens (1991), and specifically his seminal text *Modernity and Self-Identity*, is helpful here for teasing out some of the more significant changes this change in view provoked. Giddens makes an immediate distinction between pre-modern societies that are characterised by tradition, and modern societies which are post-traditional. As David Gauntlett (2008, p. 104) explains, '[when] tradition dominates, individual actions do not have to be analysed and thought about so much, because choices are already prescribed by the tradition and customs'. In opposition to this, in post-traditional societies identity is 'more mobile, multiple, personal, self-reflective, and subject to change and innovation' (Kellner 1992, p. 141). In other words self-identity 'is not a set of traits or observable characteristics. It is a person's own reflexive understanding of their biography' (Giddens 1991, p. 53). A good question at this juncture would be 'how does a person go about constructing his or her identity?' In answer to this question Giddens (1991, p. 81) proposes 'lifestyle', which he defines as being 'a more or less integrated set of practices which an individual embraces, not only because such practices fulfil utilitarian needs, but because they give material form to a particular narrative of self-identity'. So, on a daily basis each of us will make any number of outwardly unimportant decisions that pertain to a certain way of life. These decisions might include what music we listen to, how we listen to music, the football team we support, the clothes we wear, the smartphone we use, the applications we have, and so on. In each instance, the outcome of these decisions, implicitly or explicitly, says something about who we are, who we want to be, and very often, who we wish to be seen as being.

Lifestyle choices 'give our personal narrative an identifiable shape, linking us to communities of people who are 'like us' – or people who, at least, have made similar choices' (Gauntlett 2008, p. 112). Giddens (1991, p. 92) suggests this process produces a degree of 'ontological security', which is 'the confidence that most human beings have in the continuity of their self-identity and in the constancy of the surrounding social and material environment of action'. While the decisions surrounding our lifestyles might outwardly appear trivial, inwardly they can have a huge effect on our personal identity. As this is the case 'the materials' used to construct and present our various identities, 'as well as the circumstances under which this construction takes place, acquire an increased significance' (Siapera 2012, p. 173). This last point is particularly important in the context of the 'Facebook age' (Fuchs 2014), as SNS arrive with their own *imagined affordances* (Nagy and Neff 2015) that have implications for identity formation. As Nagy and Neff (2015, p. 1) explain, '*imagined affordances* emerge between users' perceptions, attitudes, and expectations; between the materiality and functionality of technologies; and between the intentions and perceptions of designers'. Regarding SNS then, *imagined affordances* may include 'digital objects like photos, videos and self-descriptions' (Belk and Ruvio 2013, p. 87) and the various meanings people attach to these items. SNS afford new ways for people to curate, present and perform who they understand themselves as 'being'. The suggestion we are making here is that identity is itself a performance played out through various platforms, such as SNS (see Hogan 2010). This echoes Goffman's (1959) understanding of the self as explained in his classic text *The Presentation of Self in Everyday Life*.

For Goffman (1959), all interactions are performances in which individuals attempt to present themselves in a certain light. 'Goffman contends that in interactions, individuals consciously contrive to give off particular expressions in order to create particular impressions in the others around them' (Peachy and Childs 2011, pp. 16–17). Consequently, identity is the outcome of enactments 'in which the actors provide an impression of the self' (Cramer et al. 2011, p. 3). As with the majority of performances, an audience is usually required:

> When an individual plays a part he implicitly requests his observers to take seriously the impression that is fostered before them. They are asked to believe that the character they see actually possesses the attributes he appears to possess, that the tasks that he performs will have the consequences that are implicitly claimed for it, and that, in general, matters are what they appear to be. (Goffman 1959, p. 28)

Taking the metaphor of the stage further still, Goffman argues that identity can readily be divided between front and back regions of social interaction, each with its own schema and corresponding subject position. Front regions are the part of the performance witnessed by the spectators. As Clarke (2008, p. 512) explains, 'if we take the principle of performance, then we may use stage props – desks, academic attire, white coats for doctors – in order to manage a 'front''. That is to say, all performances of the self are idealised (Manning 1992); actors wish to be 'shown in the best possible light to conform to cultural and societal norms' (Clarke 2008, p. 512). In stark contrast, back regions are those places 'where performers can relax and step out of character' (Ellison 2013, p. 4); those spaces where 'action occurs...related to the performance but [are] inconsistent with the appearance fostered by the performance' (Goffman 1959, p. 115). As a result of this disparity, 'it is natural to expect that the passage from the front region to the back region will be kept closed to members of the audience or that the entire back region will be hidden from them' (Goffman 1959, p. 116).

Two significant points have been made about the nature of identity that bear repeating as a means to relate this understanding to locative media. First, identity is not a passive activity; it is an active process that is the result of various life choices, and which manifest themselves in myriad ways. Second, identity can be interpreted as a performance in which people use any number of front regions to present an idealised version of themselves to others. In the digital age, one significant stage that these performances are played out on is SNS. As detailed previously, research in this vein has shown that individuals use the likes of Facebook to construct and present their identity to an audience (See Cunningham 2013; Senft 2012) with factors such as age (Livingstone 2008) and the events surrounding them (Schmalz et al. 2015) affecting what elements people choose to share. Alice Marwick's (2013) research on San Francisco's Silicon Valley nicely illustrates this point. From 2006 to 2010, Marwick (2013, p. 4) conducted an ethnographic study that explored 'how "the tech scene" [functioned], what it [valued], and what it [produced]'. Through her work Marwick quickly identified 'a strict social hierarchy. It mattered what company you worked for, whether you were an entrepreneur, and how much attention you received online' (Marwick 2013, p. 4). She also found that certain people then treated their identity as if it were a brand that they subsequently maintained through various SNS. An important *imagined affordance* in these instances was the synchronous and asynchronous messages SNS permitted (Hogan 2010). Individuals were able to choose what features of themselves they wanted to immediately share with others, just as they had the time required to respond to messages in a manner congruent with their 'brand' and that enabled them to keep '*a particular narrative going*' (Giddens 1991, p. 54).

Due to various technological advancements, and the addition of numerous features, the *imagined affordances* available through SNS have developed in numerous ways. An important example of this is the mobile social network Dodgeball (which we discussed briefly in Chapter 2), which predominately revolved around people disclosing their location to prompt social encounters. Through her research of this mobile social network, Humphreys (2007, 2010) identified a process she terms 'parochialization': by 'creating, sharing and exchanging information, social and locational', users experienced a 'sense of commonality among a group of friends in a public space' (Humphreys 2010, p. 768). That is to say, space felt more social and familiar. Following the emergence of the mobile web, location has subsequently acquired an added layer of complexity. People now use their smartphones to engage with digital information on the move, just as this information has been endowed with a sense of locality. For De Souza e Silva (2006) this development has produced what she refers to as being 'hybrid space', which occurs when physical environments are overlaid with digital information. This hybrid space is the foundation for location-based media, and location-based social networks (LBSNs) like Foursquare. As detailed in previous chapters LBSN, and broadly speaking locative media, have become the locus of a large body of research (de Souza e Silva and Frith 2012, 2015; Evans 2014; Farman 2012; Wilken and Goggin 2014). Studies have chiefly examined the impact of LBSN on space and place

(Saker 2016; Saker and Evans 2016a). This focus, however, has more recently extended to other areas, such as the impact of LBSN on sociability and social coordination (Frith 2014), memory (Frith and Kalin 2016; Kalin and Frith 2016) and significantly here the marking of one's location in the context of self-presentation (Cramer et al. 2011; Guha and Birnholtz 2013; Saker 2016; Schwartz and Halegoua 2014). While these latter example are a welcomed additional to the canon of locative media, research exploring 'practices of...impression management' (Schwartz and Halegoua 2014, p. 3) facilitated by LBSN are nonetheless still few and far between (Saker 2016). To address this shortage, Schwartz and Halegoua (2014) propose the 'spatial self' as a suitable theoretical framework for approaching such a phenomenon.

'The spatial self refers to a variety of instances (both online and offline) where individuals document, archive and display their experience and/or mobility within space in order to represent or perform aspects of their identity to others' (Schwartz and Halegoua 2014, p. 2). With the advent of locative media, the *imagined affordances* surrounding social media have moved beyond simply being textual and visual objects 'like photos, videos, and self-descriptions' (Belk and Ruvio 2013, p. 87) and now equally include 'geocoded digital traces, geographical data visualisations and maps of individual patterns of mobility'. (Schwartz and Halegoua 2014, p. 2). As Goggin (2013, p. 202) notes, 'place is a fundamental pillar of human identity' as well as 'a key category of understanding the dynamics of new media'. As a result of this, LBSN can be utilised by people to support who they understand themselves as being through the places they frequent and the connotations they assume these environments carry. It would be careless of us to suggest that people have never used the places they inhabit as part of self-expression prior to locative media, as this of course simply is not the case. To this end, Schwartz and Halegoua (2014, p. 5) readily list off a number of pre-digital instances of the spatial self, which includes photo albums, slideshows, home videos, photographic postcards (Milne 2010) as well as diaries of urban *flâneurs* stemming from the Victorian era. In each example, space is employed to suggest something meaningful about a particular period of time. This convergence of identity and place can be interpreted as communicating something meaningful about the how people are embedded in these examples. While this is correct, it is equally our assertion that the spatial self as enabled through LBSN (in this instance Foursquare) is notably different to its pre-digital predecessors. First, Foursquare enables a level of immediacy that simply was not possible before smartphones and the mobile web. Like the synchronous messages of SNS (Hogan 2010), Foursquare can be used to share a person's location instantly with a defined list of friends. Secondly, Foursquare check-ins can be witnessed by a potentially vast audience in real time. Thirdly, as discussed in the previous chapter, Foursquare has a more complex archive function and temporal dimension. Much like the asynchronous *imagined affordance* of SNS (Hogan 2010), check-ins can be stored and then algorithmically encountered at a later date for a variety of reasons. It is our suggestion that the spatial self as configured through Foursquare involves users actively thinking about the places they inhabit, what these environments might suggest about their identity and whether this is a narrative they wish to disclose to their friends or document for the future.

The aim of this chapter is therefore to examine Foursquare in light of Schwartz and Halegoua' (2014) spatial self. First, we will explore the extent to which Foursquare users comprehend one of its *imagined affordances* as revolving around the presentation of self through locality, and therefore how suitable this framework is for approaching the meanings underpinning the marking of location. Second, drawing on Giddens' (1991) understanding of the role lifestyle plays in the identity formation, we will expand upon the 'spatial self' to include identity-based practices that don't explicitly engage with the sharing of location but rather comprise the connotations associated with LBSN and digital culture. Third, we will consider what role locational suggestions (or location search) play in how users subsequently engage with their environment, and what effect this has on their sense of self.

This chapter again reports on the two original research projects designed to explore the spatial and social experience of Foursquare users. The post-research thematic analysis for this chapter involved the careful reading of full interview transcriptions, highlighting material that was of interest to the underlining research question regarding how usage related to issues of identity and self-presentation.

4.2   'I AM, WHERE I AM'

A defining feature of Foursquare its check-in function which has been shown to impact social coordination (Frith 2014) as well as giving space a sense of playfulness (Frith 2014; Saker and Evans 2016a). At the same time, the 'check-in' exceeds this and can be employed as an indicator of self. The users we spoke to were immediately aware that their check-ins communicated something more than just where they were; their spatial inscriptions communicated something about *who* they are and who they understand themselves as being:

> You choose what places you want to check-in, and this is like a creation of yourself, your identity. (Robbie)

> If you are going to a gig or whatever, you want to show off that you like that band, or you went to that gallery. (Doug)

Our research readily supports Schwartz and Halegoua (2014) 'spatial self' as an appropriate framework for exploring the use of location as a method for presenting a particular sense of self to others. For both Robbie and Doug, their shared locations are called upon to illustrate something noteworthy about the kind of people they understand themselves as being. As Robbie puts it, his check-ins are 'like a creation' of himself. Through a merging of the physical and the digital (the 'hybrid space' De Souza e Silva [2006] suggests) Foursquare has moved beyond the visual and textual markings of SNS. LBSN have an impactful *imagined affordance* of this intermingling of information and location in fashioning place as a marker of identity. Our research echoes other studies that appreciate the meanings that can the lie behind place-based performances facilitated by LBSN, and that have made similar points in the context of Foursquare and identity formation (see Cramer et al. 2011; Guha and Birnholtz 2013).

As we detailed previously, the vast majority of performances are predicated on there being an audience to observe them. The same point can be made with regard to Foursquare. In the following extract Jane discusses being aware that her check-ins might be witnessed by other people:

> So here is an interesting one between the policy and the practice. My main motivation was keep a map, tracking where I had been in 2012, you know, I went to these countries, and in England I went to these cities, and stuff like that, but then I found myself checking-in to places that I was going to pretty much a couple of times each week and stuff like that. I was in Newcastle, so I checked-in to a lot of places in Newcastle, repeatedly, so, sometimes my work place, not every day. I'd quite often check-in to the swimming pool, probably because it is good to be seen going swimming. People will check-in to the gym but won't check-in to McDonalds. (Jane)

Interestingly, Jane is conscious that she often shares when she has been swimming because it is a good thing to be *seen* doing this activity. It isn't so much the swimming itself that Jane is outwardly interested then (although this is of course part of it) but rather the realisation that could be witnessed by other people. As a consequence of this, Jane is openly mindful that her check-ins are grounded on the possibility of a corresponding audience, and that these imagined spectators might read her movements as well as the activities that take place in these locations as being in some way indicative of her identity. This sense of revealing is tethered to a particular lifestyle (Giddens 1991), one that is broadly associated with health and fitness. This position is further cemented by the next observation Jane makes, namely being that people will check-in to the gym but they won't check-in to McDonalds. Again, this underlines the reflexive application of place in relation to identity. Just as location increasingly 'provides the context from which information is interpreted and used' (de Souza e Silva and Gordon 2011, p. 12), so too does the sharing of one's locale become a practical means of constructing the *kind* of person he or she wants to be perceived as being. In the following extract, Ben develops this point further, when he discusses the impact this knowledge can have on the places he decides to share or document:

> It'll mostly be cafes and pubs that I like, maybe cinema as well, but then interestingly I probably wouldn't check-in at the Odeon. Another one might be Starbucks. I actually got berated by my sister for this as well, because I've always been quite vocal in my opposition to Starbucks. I hate the fact that it is so omnipresent. So I made the mistake of checking-in at Starbucks. I just ended up going there because a friend wanted to go there, and then got berated by my sister because of it. (Ben)

The most revealing part of this excerpt is Ben's suggestion that he 'probably' wouldn't check-in at this particular cinema, with the implicit reason for this being that he assumes it would suggest something negative about him. In a similar vein, Guha and Birnholtz (2013) have observed the 'multiple audiences' users of LBSN have to contend with whenever they are deciding whether to check-in at a particular place. An outcome of this knowledge, the authors propose, is the provision of various strategies to reduce the tension 'multiple' audiences can evoke such as the decision not to disclose one's location in the first place. The likelihood of this strategy being employed is supported by Ben's reluctance to disclose his trip to the

Odeon, as well as his pointed 'mistake' of checking-in at Starbucks and the ensuing berating he received from his sister. Much like Robbie, Doug and Jane, Ben recognises that Foursquare and its location-sharing features communicate something about his identity, which in turn leads to him engaging with his environment differently than he would outside of this LBSN. Indeed, building on Guha and Birnholtz (2013) study, our research demonstrates that Foursquare not only has the potential to alter the spaces users choose to digitally share with their friends (as established by Ben's reflections), it also has the potential to affect the kinds of places users *physically* frequent. The following extract helps cement this point, when Drew discusses the influence Foursquare can have on his behaviour:

> I'm just thinking of this one person I'm 'friends' with on Foursquare. He's friends with Katie and added me on Facebook, then added me on Foursquare. I know he probably looks at my account, and whenever I look at the [Foursquare] newsfeed I see that he's been to the gym, and it makes me think, if he's going to the gym, I should probably go to the gym. So there are certain examples where, yeah, it would influence me and I would look at other people and see what they are doing. (Drew)

There are two active processes at work in this example that warrant inspection. First, through the *imagined affordances* of Foursquare Drew is aware that his partner's friend regularly goes to the gym, and that he is accordingly the kind of person who would do this. Second, he is conscious that this person also has access to his check-ins and may therefore know that he doesn't go to the gym. For Drew, this knowledge leaves him feeling anxious that he too should probably go to the gym and in doing so become the kind of 'person' he evidently wants to be. This point is extended by Paul in the following extract:

> I had a friend who would always check-in at the gym, while I wasn't going, and it would make me feel a bit rubbish, you know, he's at the gym again, I can't believe it, he's working out a lot! So I've taken that experience and now I'm checking-in, so I feel better. I guess for some reason checking-in on it made it feel a bit more like I'd actually been, because people knew I'd been, rather than just going on my own. You know, people could go four or five times a week, not check in, and you'd never know. For some reason, if I check in and everyone sees he's at the gym again, it feels a bit more like I've done something. (Paul)

In this instance, Paul intriguingly details a desire to not only go to the gym but also for his gym check-ins to be witnessed by others. Paul suggests that it is through this 'witnessing' that the reality of his movements then feel more real. This observation provides another thought-provoking position on the affective character of the spatial self as configured through Foursquare. In employing Foursquare as a digital platform from which he might potentially be observed, Paul not only adapts his spatial movements but also looks for a certain degree of spatial surveillance. Paul's check-ins are performed with two apparent motives in mind. First, they are a marker of his movements. Second, they offer a vicarious viewpoint on the identity he wants to project. Sarah outlines a similar purpose for her check-ins:

> I'm registered disabled, with the M.E. and I'm mainly housebound. So Foursquare was just an incentive to get out and get mayorships, and to tell friends and family that I'm out, rather than having to ring them and say I'm at such and such a place today, they can instantly see, when I published my check-ins, where I was and that I was getting out. It kept them happy because they were concerned I wasn't getting out, you know, cabin fever and just wasting away in the house. It's really brightened them up to see that I'm getting out and about. (Sarah)

For Sarah then, aside from the appeal of Foursquare's game mechanics which includes points, badges and mayorships, there an equally important *imagined affordance* of this LBSN is that it lets her friends and family know she is 'getting out' and not just 'wasting away in the house'. This affordance also has implication for how Sarah perceives herself:

> Yeah it is a big part of my identity, which is why I particularly wanted something about it at the wedding, because Foursquare is me, it's such a big part of my life, it's made such a big impact on my life, I felt that if I had something Foursquare involved, it would be more personal. (Sarah)

As Sarah states with some impact, 'Foursquare is me'. Sarah doesn't simply use Foursquare to communicate that she has left the house although this is of course part of it. More importantly, her usage allows Sarah to identify with a version of herself which isn't rooted in M.E. but is instead seen as being physically active. This sense of self is then further strengthened through the various social connections Foursquare opens up:

> It gives me something to talk about that isn't my M.E. Sometimes I just get bored of saying, I didn't go out yesterday, and I didn't go out the day before, you know, I was stuck in bed the day before that. It is just something different to talk about. I'll tell my friends what badges I unlocked, or something like that. Some of them aren't remotely interested. If I could talk about it all day I know I would. (Sarah)

Here, our research demonstrates it that the use of location through Foursquare is evidently different to the likes of Dodgeball, which predominately functioned to facilitate social interactions (Humphreys 2007, 2010). In the series of previous examples, Foursquare is in part employed to perpetuate a certain sense of self rooted in the various connotations associated with particular environments. As a result of this, users spend more time thinking about the spaces they inhabit, what these places might say about them and the different audiences they present their location to through using LBSN. Users adopt suitable strategies to contend with the multiple audiences they might face, including the decision not checking-in to a certain environment, or to avoid these places all together. And lastly, owing to the knowledge that their check-ins might be witnessed by potential audiences, users are able to strengthen their projected self-presentation through the vicarious subject positions these digital imprints of location make on other people.

4.3   THE SPATIAL SELF ISN'T ALWAYS, WELL, SPATIAL

So far we have explored an assortment of instances where Foursquare involves users performing and affirming who they understand themselves as 'being' by sharing and documenting their day-to-day movements. At the same time however, our research also discovered that the spatial self as configured through Foursquare does not necessarily have to be spatial but can instead revolve around the lifestyles with which this practice is associated. For the most part, this lifestyle revolves around new technologies:

> We're both very much internet people. I've got Tweet Deck running on my phone; I've got Tweet Deck running on my laptop in the office; it is also running on my laptop at home. When I go for a cigarette I am probably reading foursquare or Twitter. (Adrian)

I think I just read about it somewhere, and thought that sounds like something I'd be interested in. I'm into all of this kind of stuff anyway, new gadgets, technologies and apps. I'm all over it anyway. So I'll hear about something and think that sounds cool let's try it out. (Nigel)

As Nigel notes, his interest in Foursquare is symptomatic of a broader interest in 'new gadgets, technologies and apps' as well as a desire to try these technologies out. This was a lifestyle indicator shared by many of the users we spoke to:

Okay, so at university I studied television production, I now work with Apple, the retail store, and I've always been very 'techie' and into your kind of social media and sort of web technologies in a way. I dabbled in web design myself. So yeah, it's always been something that has attracted me really. (Paul)

I guess I've been interested in it before phones had GPSs. So while I was at Southampton I was quite interested in the idea of checking-in or some kind of location-based game. I tried very hard with a friend at Southampton to make something like that. It was in the days of smartphones running Java and things like that – before Android – and trying to get it to talk to a Bluetooth GPS, and all kinds of crazy things like that. So I was quite excited when the technology caught up. So yeah, initially I was playing Gowalla, and then moved onto foursquare. I guess it does kind of highlight my interests. I'm interested in maps and location and things. I'm interested in technology and gadgets and things. (Ryan)

Significantly here, Nigel (an Information Technology [IT] Support Team Manager), Paul (an Apple Store Genius) and Ryan (a Technical Architect for the BBC) all have occupations that revolve around technology and each reference these connections when discussing their association Foursquare. This is also the case with John, whose job in the IT industry meant he grew up with new technologies. There is a lifestyle that this kind of history implicitly refers to, which in John's mind goes some way towards explaining his use of this LBSN:

Well, probably the most pertinent fact would be that I worked for IBM for thirty-seven years, and working in the IT industry, with computers as an emerging industry, I started work obviously before there were any PCs or mobile phones, or anything like that, so I sort of grew up with that technology and really developed an interest in the new technologies as they emerged. I tended to work with younger people. I was probably old enough to be their dad. In later life I worked in IT support, and the people I worked with were very young, and I think that influenced me a great deal because they were always very keen on new technologies, and I tended to go along with them. When the new mobile phones came out I was quite interested in them. I haven't had one for very long, because I just never got around to getting one, but then I was bought one for my birthday and I have been using it for well over a year and a half, and yeah, I'm interested in all technologies really, computers, cameras, mobile phones, anything of that ilk. (John)

For Doug too, it is his role teaching Digital Media with the kind of commitments this position entails that eventually led to him signing up to Foursquare:

I tend to sign up to every social network going, because of my job. Gowalla sounded a little more interesting because I quite like the idea of reality and the social network coming together. So unlike Twitter where it doesn't really have any impact, this was focused on merging these two aspects, which I thought was quite interesting. Some of it is off of the back of this old Carnegie Mellon talk by this guy, I can't remember his name, about gamifying a lot of general process, like going on a bus and getting points etcetera, he goes in to this whole thing, a lot of it is about Facebook, and I was kind of interested in this just generally, so it was just a service that I thought sounded interesting, so I joined Gowalla, which was pretty cool. Obviously Foursquare was coming along at the same time. I just didn't think Foursquare was as good. (Doug)

When it comes to identity, continuity is understandably an important part of the phenomenon as it is precisely through continuity that the past is explained and 'orientated towards an anticipated future' (Gauntlett 2008, p. 108). An 'anticipated' future can readily be recognised in the various research extracts detailed previously, as users evidently comprehend their connection with Foursquare as being a natural progression in the context of their individual biographies. In addition our research also found was that users, rightly or wrongly, held strong beliefs about how their friends viewed them and what social expectations they therefore faced:

All my friends know I like to be in touch with up-and-coming things like that, and foursquare is a very up-and-coming thing. I've thought so for the past two and a half years. So far so good. I think if I didn't know about foursquare I don't think that would be right, because foursquare has been a big thing, and it's been up-and-coming for a while, and I think it is something people will think: he'll know about Foursquare. (Mark)

In a similar way, John's use of Foursquare is also as a result of the expectations he feels his friends have of him as the 'person with a smartphone'. This expectation then becomes reflexively intertwined with his own sense of self as well a feature that effectively marks him out from his retired peers:

> When we're out and about, you know, and I'm using my phone, and I'm using it in a social media situation, that to my friends is a pain. When they say to me, we need a restaurant, can you go on your mobile phone and find a local restaurant, or we need petrol where is the nearest garage, then suddenly the smartphone becomes a useful tool, so that is my sort of my identity, the person with the smartphone. (John)

'To be a "person" is not just to be a reflexive actor, but to have a concept of a person (as applied both to the self and others)' (Giddens 1991, p. 53). For Mark, this means that it would be 'wrong' if he didn't use Foursquare as he comprehends himself as being identified by his association with up-and-coming technologies. Our research demonstrates that Foursquare provides users with another means of extending or affirming themselves and their self-image precisely through these expectations. John comments that his friends in part identify him through his smartphone, which has become a significant part of his story. As Giddens (1991, p. 54) explains:

> The individual's biography, if she is to maintain regular interaction with others in the day-to-day world, cannot be wholly fictive. It must continually integrate events which occur in the external world, and sort them into the ongoing 'story' about the self.

For both Mark and John, the expectations they experience from their friends are explicitly integrated into their ongoing narratives, which then allows them to reinforce further their respective selves through the practice of using Foursquare. Alongside the perpetuation these personal narrative in the manner detailed previously, our research also illustrates that

Foursquare can provide users with the opportunity to connect with communities of people who share similar lifestyles, which has implications for the cohesiveness of their identities:

> I've met some really interesting people online. I wouldn't say they'd all be my best friends or my drinking buddies, but they're good to have a chat to when you're bored late at night and there is nothing on television, or you can't be bother to read that night; there's always someone on Twitter or someone in the forum that you can have some banter and a laugh and a joke with. There's just a small group of us and we get on really well. (Dennis)

> It is nice to have that little circle of people that I can literally rabbit about foursquare with, all day. I am bonkers about foursquare. I don't know why I've got the enthusiasm that I have? I just appreciate it so much, as it has changed my life; it has got me out the house so much more than what I used to. So I've just got this big appreciation for it. (Sarah)

Interestingly, in the latter excerpt the 'circle' of friends Sarah alludes to is geographically dispersed. This is a situation that many of the users who employed Foursquare in this way experienced. However, this isn't to suggest that Foursquare can't or doesn't lead to physical encounters, as Dennis explains:

> I have in the sense of, like this guy Ian, I had no idea who he was, then I got a message saying he'd stolen my mayorship, and then I saw his Twitter, and tweeted him to say, give that back, and then you just get chatting, and it has got to the point where we've gone for one drink. I wouldn't say we were going to be best friends. (Dennis)

This last point is significant, as '[while] television, telephone, and internet research have shown the importance of media to build new social connections... there has been relatively little research exploring how mobile technology may also serve this function' (Humphreys 2008, p. 115). For some users, by associating with this particular lifestyle, Foursquare not only confirms their identity but equally provides new social opportunities that then similarly feed back into their ongoing stories of self. In summary then, our research illustrates that the spatial self can be extended to practices that don't strictly engage with spatiality, but that revolve around the formation and maintenance of identity nonetheless.

4.4   LOCAL SEARCH AND FEELING 'LOCAL'

An important element of Foursquare is the locational suggestions (or location search) it can provide. This feature involves algorithmically drawing together users' historical check-ins to make place-based suggestion that are congruent with the user's history when they are seeking locative inspiration, such as a place to eat. From the beginning, this function was heavily promoted as offering a different kind of tool for exploring space (Cramer et al. 2011; Frith 2013). In association with this understanding, many of the users we spoke to primarily used Foursquare as a viable way of navigating their environment. As Robbie explains:

> It has just given me an insight into exciting places I should go. (Robbie)

In the following extract and while thinking about how Foursquare has changed the way he approaches going out, Terry details a similar situation:

> As corny as this may sound when me and Lucy are thinking where we shall go for lunch or dinner, I don't have that problem anymore; I'm guided by foursquare. You can look at what is around you and go here, here and here, and I think that's great. I don't have that thing where you end up going to the same place over and over again. If you do it, it is because you get value for money, not because you are just bored. (Terry)

This kind of use is also demonstrated by Henry in the following text. Henry, having recently moved to London, uses this LBSN to help him familiarise himself with an otherwise unfamiliar city:

> I don't use foursquare with the intention of letting people know where I am right now, so they can find me, nor do I use it to see where people are. That's not the reason why I use it. I like to use it when I check in so I can learn about new places to go for dinner, and stuff like that, but not to stalk people. (Henry)

Mark makes a similar point while discussing his use of Foursquare during a physics trip to Geneva. Again, it should be note here that Mark's reflexive awareness of his own identity is immediately apparent in his language:

> I had a physics trip to Geneva to see LHC, and we were there and everyone was like I don't know where we should go to night and I was like, this is a

job for me then, and found a really good *crêperie* nearby, and we went there, and everyone had about five *crêpes* because they were so good. So that was good. (Mark)

What the previous excerpts demonstrate is that Foursquare provides these users with place-based information that effects where they go and what they do. At the same time there is of course more to this process than simply the provision of locational information, as such information could readily be accessed from a variety of sources that aren't necessarily locative or indeed digital. For these users, Foursquare evidently offers them something that they trust in terms of suggesting which places they should visit. Indeed, there is an implicit and unerring belief in the nature of the recommendations Foursquare delivers. Owing to this, these users are interminably confident that by employing Foursquare they are able to access to a city that would otherwise be hidden from them; a city that is cordoned off from those who aren't in the know, as it were. The following extracts helps further develop this point:

In London there was a completely hidden, random dim sum restaurant that I found. It was down a small street in China Town that you wouldn't know about because the back entrance is where the restaurant is, and there's just a small door, and there it is. (David)

During the Olympics I was over in South London, I tend not to go south of the river very often, I hate to say it, and literally opened the 'explore' feature and just started searching for restaurants, within a mile, and found the most amazing tapas restaurant [José] I have been to in my life, just based on the fact so many people had recommended it. That was my hidden gem. (Amy)

In many ways this place [favourite café] is a hidden gem. It is almost as if you are a secret member of the Foursquare club. (Richard)

I was on holiday recently. I went to Malaga and didn't necessarily know that much about it. For trying to find places to eat that weren't tourist hotspots, Foursquare was perfect. So you could do the 'explore' option and say that you wanted somewhere to eat and then it would give me a list of places that are popular on Foursquare, and obviously people on Foursquare are more likely to be locals than tourists, or so I assumed. So it made it a lot easier to try and find places. I think they must have been local people, because most of the tips were in Spanish and I couldn't understand any of them. (Ben)

Another important element of LBSN use then is the faith that its locative suggestions are written by people who really know the areas, further cementing the suggestion that this information couldn't be accessed through other channels. Whether this is accurate or not is of course impossible to know. Furthermore, the veracity of this belief is inconsequential. Instead, what matters, and what we want to focus on here, is that it is precisely through this belief that these users are able to experience a city that subsequently *feels* different. Humphreys' (2007, 2010) research on Dodgeball and specifically the process she terms 'parochialization', which materialises when the social sentience enabled through this mobile social networks makes users feel like they are interminably inhabiting familiar environments, provides a nuanced way of examining the impact of Foursquare on space, place and indeed, identity. Regarding Foursquare, it is our assertion that local recommendations do not so much make space feel different, or 'parochial', but alters how *users* themselves feel in these environments. When using the local search function users believe they are privy to locational information which is itself 'local'. By utilising this information, these users are subsequently able to take on a subject position that *feels* similarly local, and that then impacts their experience of space:

It feels more like getting the insider's view on the local area because it is the people that live there that are most likely to be checking-in regularly and posting tips for places. (Ben)

The 'tips' are probably my favourite thing about Foursquare. You do just get the inside deal from regular users that go there, that say, don't try this or do try that. It doesn't feel as daunting or scary as when you go somewhere and stare at the menu thinking, oh god what shall I have, and that kind of thing. (Sarah)

The standout experience I had was in Paris. We went to one of the museums, and it was the day that we were going home, so time was tight, and it was in the morning. So we got there and the queue was literally zigzagging. So I was standing in the queue and I thought I'll check-in and while I was standing there I was reading the tips and one of them said the queue is massive, however, if you go around the corner you'll find the queue for the library, which gets you in the same place, in terms of the ticketing area, and there is hardly anyone in that cue, so go to that cue and you will beat the main queue. I almost felt like we were committing an offence. (Nigel)

Now I don't go to McDonalds often, but it was with the kids so it was a treat, so this is a McDonalds based story; the tip on it said that a particular member of staff, who must have had a badge, was like really horrible, and it was kind of a bit weird, because then I knew a secret there, because I'm thinking that member of staff probably isn't on Foursquare, they don't know I am here, and I'm now watching them. It does give you a more authentic experience, although authentic is such a terrible word. (Doug)

Regarding Schwartz and Halegoua (2014) notion of the spatial self then, the use of local search suggests a different relationship between identity and place as well as a different relationship between Goffman's (1959) front and back regions. Take Paul's gym check-ins for instance; these inscriptions were explicitly motivated by a desire to perform the kind of person Paul wanted to be seen as 'being'. In performing this practice, Paul is able to present himself in this fashion and he is also able to have this identity affirmed through the imagined audience that might witness any one of his accumulative enactments. This process then has a marked effect on the 'passage from the front region to the back region, which Goffman (1959, p. 116) suggests is 'kept closed to members of the audience' (Goffman 1959, p. 116). For Paul, the witnessing by others of his movements enables him to distance himself gradually from the performative side of his identity. As a symptom of this distancing, the 'passage from the front region to the back region' (Goffman 1959, p. 116) is then closed to Paul too. As a consequence, the performed identity Paul observes through his Foursquare use ceases to be a performance and instead becomes his identity. In contrast, the users in the examples detailed previously aren't necessarily engaging with locational recommendations to disseminate a certain sense of self but are instead interested in gaining access to a place-based experience that would otherwise be concealed from them. However, by engaging with this kind of information and when considered alongside the belief this information is indigenous, their self-identities are altered. While Paul believes his front stage performance is indicative of his back region, users like Nigel and Ben are very aware of the difference between these two stages. Furthermore, it is precisely through this difference between the two stages that Nigel and Ben are able to adopt subject positions that momentarily feel authentically 'local'.

Our research also provides a more nuanced take on perhaps why Ben didn't want to be identified with the Odeon or Starbucks. An important function of Foursquare for some of the users we spoke to was that it supposedly helped them avoid places that they deemed to lack a certain genuineness. This function was particularly important to these users because they similarly understood themselves as being the kind of people who frequented places that weren't commercial chains, but were more 'real' or 'authentic' than this. Again, the veracity of this faith is inconsequential. What is important is that these users believed it, and that this belief then impacted how they used Foursquare. For these users then, another important *imagined affordance* of this LBSN was that it offered some locative protection against their supposedly authentic identities being threatened by places that lacked the same degree of authenticity. By then marking themselves as present in these places, users' identities were then further reinforced.

4.5   FOURSQUARE AND THE SPATIAL SELF IT CONFIGURES

This chapter has examined the various ways in which one's physical movements alongside the use of LBSN that may take place in these environments can be used to perpetuate a certain sense of self. This began with an examination of the *imagined affordances* of SNS, and the various ways SNS are used by people to 'present a highly curated version of themselves' (Schwartz and Halegoua 2014, p. 3) before moving on to important advancements, including smartphones and the mobile web, which has led to location being incorporated into social networking sites. Locative media and LBSN such as Foursquare have immediate implications for questions that pertain to identity formation, as borne out by our research. Indeed, the Foursquare users we spoke to were immediately aware that their check-ins connoted something meaningful about the kind of people they are, which had the potential to be witnessed by different audiences. As a result of this, for many of the users their check-ins weren't something that they simply did on a whim without thinking about factors such as where they were and what this place might suggest about their identity but was rather a process that demanded more deliberation and thought. For these users Foursquare became a platform that could be called upon to present facets of their identity through the environments they frequented (Guha and Birnholtz 2013). As a 'theoretical framework' then 'that explores the presentation of the self, based on geographic traces of physical activity' (Schwartz and Halegoua 2014, p. 5), the spatial self was readily supported by our research. As Cramer et al. (2011, p. 9) argue, '[ultimately], what this means is that location has changed from being something you *have* (a property or state) to something you *do* (an action)'.

Drawing on Goffman's (1959) suggestion that identity is itself a performance divided between front and back regions, Foursquare is a viable platform for enacting one's sense of self. What is most important about the various self-presentations discussed throughout this chapter is the way in which users utilised their respective spatial stages to perform a version of themselves that they were then able to believe in, precisely because of the digital traces these performances left behind. Foursquare and the *imagined affordances* that relate to identity formation seemingly infuse these self-projections with a measure of validity that simply isn't possible without the incorporation of location, and the vicarious legitimacy this outwardly brings in its wake. For users like Paul and Sarah they were at once both performer and spectator of their own Foursquare feeds, with the division between front and back regions effectively closed in the process. By keeping this passage locked, Paul and Sarah were able to suspend any disbelief they may have had about the reality of their identities. In other words, and while continuing to use Goffman's (1959) terminology, as a symptom of Foursquare and the spatial self it configures the division between front and back stage is gradually erased until the point there is no division to speak of. It is precisely through this process that the spatial self of Foursquare enabled users to present identities that then felt more real.

For Humphreys (2010, p. 775) an important feature of mobile social media like Dodgeball, and the social thinking they enable, is that they 'make the urban environment [seem] less cold and anonymous'. In relation to LBSN then, it isn't simply that Foursquare increased the sociability of space, although this is part of it (Frith 2014); equally Foursquare enabled users to further embed their identities into the various spaces they frequented on a daily basis. Put differently, for the users we spoke to Foursquare meant that they could present a sense of self that exhibited a degree of locational consistency with regard to the perceived character of places that they checked-into. Building on research within this field that has observed LBSN being employed to present the self through location (Guha and Birnholtz 2013) then, our research significantly demonstrates that Foursquare can in fact alter the places a person goes, with a view to establishing a sense of self that is reliable and consistent. To be clear, we are not suggesting that all Foursquare check-ins are 'real' or 'authentic' in this sense, as user can of course check-in to places where they are not physically located or check-in to an incongruous place. However, for the most part the users that we engaged share a similar belief that user check-ins should be accurate, as anything else goes against the 'spirit' of Foursquare.

Just as this chapter sought to employ the 'spatial self' as a lens through which to consider the various uses of Foursquare, our research also demonstrated that this framework can be extended in two ways. First, the spatial self isn't always as spatial as its eponymous title. For the Foursquare users we spoke to, their use of Foursquare wasn't simply something that had happened out of the blue but was rather part and parcel of a much bigger narrative that they had been developing over a period of time. This narrative revolved around a particular lifestyle, which as Giddens (1991) points out is an important indicator of a person's identity. In this instance, the lifestyle in question comprised new technologies and an interest in gadgets. Many users explained that they had become involved in Foursquare through this lifestyle choice, with their affirmed inclination for new technologies enabling their identities to be effectively continued. In addition to this, these users also strongly believed that their friends perceived them in a manner as people who would use LBSN, and thus they felt in some ways obligated to engage with Foursquare. We also established the location recommendations Foursquare provides do not simply alter the places uses go, but also impact how these users feel about themselves in these places. Through a belief in the 'indigenous' character (i.e. user generated) of the locational recommendations Foursquare provides, these users were able to experience space in a manner that felt 'local'. This accordingly enabled them to fleetingly adopt a commensurate subject position of 'being local'. Interestingly here, users did not enact these locative suggestions (front stage) to influence themselves (back stage) – quite the opposite in fact. Nonetheless, it was precisely through these performances, and a stark awareness of them being a performance, that these users momentarily were able to experience a sense of self that felt unerringly 'authentic'.

CHAPTER 5

Conclusions

Abstract The final chapter reiterates the conclusions on spatiality, temporality and identity and considers these findings in the context of other research findings and theory in the area. This chapter also surveys the area of LBSN as it stands and positions the current project in terms of LBSN research and social media research in general. The conclusions of both this research and research in the area are used to critically assess the nature of current LBSN in the context of how places, users and identity are represented, mediated and framed by the applications. This chapter also considers how the features of LBSN identified in this work may be utilised in future applications and locative media. That the key aspects of LBSN will be further developed in the future is inevitable due to the political economy of data production in LBSN, which provide rich data for targeted advertising. This political economy gives LBSN the status of 'zombie' media that will go on to influence the form of other SNS into the future.

Keywords Political economy of LBSN · Databases of place · Data · Zombie media

As we stated in the introduction, we had four main aims or points in mind when setting out this book. Firstly, we wanted to offer a brief historical account of the development and uptake of LBSN, with a

© The Author(s) 2017   87
L. Evans, M. Saker, *Location-Based Social Media*,
DOI 10.1007/978-3-319-49472-2_5

consideration of why so many LBSN didn't enjoy the mainstream success of other more established social media. We'll address that latter point in this conclusion. Secondly, this related closely to the 'death' of LBSN. Here, we will argue that LBSN is not a form of 'dead media', but instead can be thought of as a form of 'zombie media' that animates and haunts other media platforms. Thirdly, we wanted this book to be read as a literature review of the main academic approaches and work on LBSN, which we hope the four previous chapters have achieved. Finally, the most important part of this book was the three chapters that detailed the effects of LBSN use on spatiality, identity and temporality. We will summarise these findings briefly here, with the intention of opening up this research into a discussion of where LBSN use and research currently is and where it will be in the future.

5.1   SUMMARY OF THE RESEARCH

It is perhaps an exercise in futility to simply reiterate what we hope you have already read in this book. However, futile as it may be it is still worthwhile to recap on the main findings of this research in order to draw this survey of LBSN together. In Chapter 2, we argued that the mechanics of the LBSN Foursquare altered how people move through their environment. The elements of LBSN are used to affirm users' sense of localness in space and to create a new relationship to places through active spatiality. Playfulness (or the gamification of location) accentuates sociability and familiarity with places. Spatiality as an appreciation of everyday spaces around users was approached in a novel way through the use of LBSN in playful and habitual ways. Chapter 3 dealt with the temporal aspects of the use of LBSN, and identified these applications as 'mediated memory objects' (Van Dijck 2009). We argued that LBSNs work to preserves the past in a manner that feels 'secure and enduring'. This feature of the application structures the use of LBSN in the present (i. e. people check-in to preserve their location in the future) and anticipates a nostalgic, history-based use of the application in the future as people look to recover and reminisce over their movements that have been encoded in the databases of the application. In Chapter 4, these spatial and temporal aspects were consolidated in a discussion of identity, where the evidence from our ethnographic research indicated that LBSN users integrate their use of the application into ongoing narrative accounts of their lives. Choices of locations to check-into are used to augment and give salience to these impressions of identity, working to reinforce self-identity and project idealised identities to connections across social networks.

This survey of the research cannon on LBSN and our original ethnographic research was partially motivated by a desire to show that these applications were not mere time-wasting services, something used when bored senseless or by the more eager over-sharers in modern society. The use of LBSN, for some users of these services, resulted in some profound experiential changes for spatiality, temporality and identity. The research we have detailed provides ample support for other research findings that we have discussed in the course of this book. In terms of spatiality, we have found that particular uses of LBSN can alter engagement with space, in agreement with research on locative media by Hjorth (2012) and Farman (2012) amongst many others while contesting the notion of the spatial separateness of play (Huizinga 1938/1992). We leaned heavily on Lefebvre's (1974/1991) insistence on the importance of location to understanding spatiality, and the notion of embodiment with regard to using LBSN as an embedded part of everyday life for these users. These theoretical positions could be used across other analyses of mobile media use, social media use in different locations and media usage in general. On temporality, our phenomenologically informed approach offered support for the notion of media technologies such as LBSN being structuring influences on time and memory. The importance of LBSN can be seen as contributing location in a very explicit way to this inorganic organisation of memory. Such an approach has been fruitful across media and technology studies, and our research here supports much of the key theoretical work from the likes of Chun (2011) and Stiegler (1998) amongst others. We see these effects in other prominent applications like Snapchat's new Memories function, Facebook's 'on this day' feature and the application Timehop. Finally, the work on identity detailed in Chapter 4 acts as a subject-specific adaptation of the theoretical approaches of Goffman (1959), Giddens (1991) and Schwarz and Halegoua (2014). The performance of identity, maintenance of identity over time and 'spatial self' were all influenced by the use of LBSN. For the users of LBSN in our research the visible use of the applications and the projection of location both became salient indicators of identity over time.

So, far from being a fatuous waste of time, LBSN have in actuality had a rather profound effect on some extremely important facets of being human for those that used them in their everyday lives. Which begs an incredibly important question: why did LBSN fail so badly, if the effects of using them are so 'profound'?

5.2   THE ROLE OF LBSN IN THE WORLD

Given the mainstream failure of stand-alone LBSN but the increasing use of LBSN features in other popular social networks, it is fairly important to analyse the shortcomings of LBSN applications and the reasons why their key functions are being retained and integrated into other platforms such as Facebook and Twitter. The failure of these platforms can be attributed to their limited social value or capital but the social capital that can be attributed to location is part of the reason that they live on in other forms and in other platforms. Of more importance is the political economy of these applications, and the value that this provides which gives a very compelling reason as to why these applications have been integrated into other social networking services.

It might sound extreme to suggest that these applications failed, with Foursquare still being an active application installed by over 60 million people globally. As we detailed in the introduction to this book though, many services such as Brightkite, Gowalla, SCVNGR, Loopt, Sonar and Rummble have long departed the app stores of the digital age. At best, we can claim that these services have influenced the development of features of other services. A very simple explanation as to why they diminished in a short time would be to point to their limited application. Location alone and the sharing of location (even in a game environment) offers a very limited affordance in terms of social media. In the context of social media, we know that these affordances are a major part of everyday life. As Baym (2015, p. 110) notes, social media and new technologies in general offer a many affordances that influence what happens in the world because of these affordances. The mediation of the world through new technologies is interwoven, not juxtaposed, with everything else in the world. As Sophocles said many years before Nancy Baym wrote, 'nothing vast enters the lives of mortals without a curse'. The continual checking of social media, posting of inanities and structuring of activities around the news-feed and messages enabled by social media are perhaps the 'curse' (or indeed the blessing) in this context. While we do not argue that LBSN are as critical as other SNS in terms of their effect on the world because of the relative lack of affordances that they offered (and hence this being an important aspect of their demise), the co-opting of the affordances that they did and still do have in some cases mean that they remain an important footnote in the history of social media studies and digital media studies in general.

To clarify this, we can think of what one can do on the behemoth social media juggernaut Facebook. One can post a status; share a photo; tag a photo; share a video; play a poorly coded flash game; send a message; chat in real time; post a note; like another person's status, photo, video; add a friend; delete a friend; join a page; make a page; like a page; plan an event; indicate attendance at an event; and loads of other things including checking-into a place like a LBSN. While the LBSNs that bloomed from 2010 to 2012 could do some of these things, they could not include all of the affordances of Facebook, and indeed Facebook could offer the affordances of LBSN and more. While Twitter has more limited affordances, its niche messaging style obviously offered something more attractive than gamified locational posting. What our research has indicated is that the people that were most enthusiastic users of LBSN were people that recognised modern life as a technologically textured existence (Ihde 1990, p. 1), and adapted their use of LBSN into this appreciation and perspective on life. For many, Facebook will suffice as it conveniently affords the features of other SNS in one platform. So LBSN have been, in a manner of speaking, consumed by the larger SNS platforms. It is not only LBSN that suffered this fate; take for example other niche social networks such as GetGlue (for 'checking-into' television programmes or events), the original hype machine Myspace, or the original SNS of them all Friendster. The features of these SNS have been cherry-picked by other SNS over the years to create the platforms that we are most familiar with today. While we do not see the often retina-damaging HTML experiments of Myspace profile design on Facebook, we do see the visible friend lists, news feeds and profile walls all still in place. We can discuss and like a television programme a la GetGlue, and build a community of friends like Friendster afforded us the opportunity to do. As Arthur (2009) argues in tracing the evolution of technologies, new technologies are not strictly speaking inventions. They do not come from nowhere. All new technology is created from existing technology and that existing technology fades into the background of the world in which the new technology shines. However, that old technology is not gone forever as it is still playing its part in the shaping of the world through its presence in new forms.

We are positioning LBSN here in a way that marks them as one of Thomas Hughes' (1983) *reverse salients*. Hughes' used this term to refer to old technologies that interrupt and disturb the forward movement of technology. In the case of LBSN we have a series of social networking sites that had their time, failed but still influence and permeate the new or continually advancing major SNS that dominate the social media environment. The most salient features of LBSN (the check-in and sharing of location across the network) have been integrated either verbatim into SNS (such as Facebook's Places feature, no doubt assisted by their purchase of Gowalla) or in modified form such as location-bearing tweets on Twitter's mobile application. The 'old' technology continues to be a feature of the new and developing technology, and location-based features should be assumed to be a critical part of whatever new SNS will emerge from these current leaders in the market. This of course precedes any reflection on how the current SNS are harvesting data on location as part of their marketing and advertising platforms. It is perhaps here that we find the most salient reasons for the retaining of the key features of LBSN in SNS and other digital media platforms.

Back in 2013, one of the authors of this book (Evans 2013) wrote a short piece on how Foursquare as an application was leveraging the free labour of its users to build a potentially massive and lucrative database of location for advertisers. This political economy argument balanced on the proposition that as users' checked-into places, the check-in data could be broken down into activity, location, time and frequency of visiting, companions and who this information was shared with to build individually based locational profiles of users that could be used for targeted advertising by the actual customers of LBSN – the advertisers. It is always worth reminding ourselves that the customers of all social media i.e. those that pay to use social media are the advertisers that pay for access to the users of a particular SNS. As Fuchs (2014, p. 22) outlines, in capitalist societies culture is always linked very closely to the notion of the commodity. Cultural commodities are always being bought and sold by consumers, and media consumers are bought and sold themselves as an audience (see Smythe 1977). Advertising and the commodification of humans that use social media is an essential mechanism of SNS to drive business – the average value of each of Facebook's 1.59 billion users in the final quarter of 2015 was $3.79 per user, accounting for revenues of $5.84 billion in that period (Gibbs 2016). The process of packaging up the data on users and their preferences for advertisers is automatic, with sophisticated algorithms aggregating and flattening users into easily packaged forms much like Credit Default Options did for mortgages prior to the 2008 financial crash. This is a model driven on activity, as to have a profile that can be broken down for advertisers one must contribute to that profile; likes, posts and photos equal cash.

Without this discussion becoming overly pessimistic and alienating, the argument for LBSN being one of the more valuable commodity forms of social networking is fairly straightforward. What could an advertiser want more than to know where you go, what you do there and what time you go there and who you go there with? This accumulation of valuable information into data to be sold was predicted in 2013 (Evans 2013) to be the key to LBSN business models and their progress after the burst of users tapered off. That this information was all user-generated and therefore zero-cost to the LBSN itself was seen as the key aspect of this business model. Get 50 million people to contribute information on their movements for free, then sell on that information to advertisers? Profit. However, things have not exactly followed that simple path to commodity nirvana. The failure of many stand-alone LBSN can be traced to the fact that they could not effectively monetise their platform. The reasons for this are many, from a lack of planning to controversies over the privacy implications of selling off highly granular locational data to advertisers. Important to this discussion though is the nature of the data that these applications and platforms produced. As Haklay (2013, p. 55) argued, all neo-geographical applications (which LBSN could be considered an example of as a data-producing and using software) are value-bound in particular ways. Here, we are arguing that LBSN applications are coded in a way that embodies a particular set of values, or if you like looks to build the idea of value into their operations. Haklay (2013, p. 55) argued that there are particular limits to neo-geographical applications that limit them but it is most important to note that these values are non-democratic and may break free in new forms. The logic or value of LBSN then is one where value can be derived from use of the application, and that use is the mobility and activity of users as they decide to mark their location.

The idea of this value breaking free in new forms is interesting when we consider the trajectory of the data of LBSN following the reduction in use of these applications post-2012. The well-documented purchase of Gowalla by Facebook is one example of this migration of value-laden data to another platform, but this may be too crude and blunt an example for our purposes here, interesting though it clearly is. To explore this notion of value 'breaking-through' on other platforms or being realised in transformations to other platforms we can use two very recent examples of the use, integration and sale of Foursquare data. In March 2016, Twitter announced a 'partnership' with Foursquare to use the Foursquare databases to have the option to label a tweet with a specific business, landmark, or point of interest (Shah 2016). These locational tags can then be followed through a timeline of tweets that include the locational tag. These 'places' are sourced from Foursquare. The places that were created by Foursquare users and collated into a database of place (Evans 2015, p. 38) can now be accessed by Twitter users to label their tweets with a location. While the precise financial details of the partnership between the two social media applications is not known, the fact that Twitter is using a bespoke database of places rather than developing their own through user-generated activity is interesting. To do such a thing, Twitter would need to disrupt their own user-interfaces and add functionality to their relatively simple social media offering. Instead, using Foursquare's database (built on the free labour of Foursquare users) allows Twitter to integrate quickly a massive database of locations into their platform with minimal disruption. In essence, Twitter adds value to their platform through the use of value accrued and derived from Foursquare and its users. A similar development has been seen with a link-up between Foursquare and the controversially disruptive ride provider Uber. In May 2016, Uber announced that it would incorporate Foursquare's places into its application to allow users to select places as from Foursquare's Point of Interest (POI) database as a start point or destination for your journey (Buczkowski 2016). The expressed aim of this integration is to enable drivers and users to find exact locations more easily. Additional value can be found in the fact that any modifications in the POI database will be incorporated into Foursquare's venue database in the future to improve accuracy and efficacy. What is clear from these examples is that Foursquare is no longer just a LBSN, but sees itself as a big data provider for other social networking sites and digital media-based enterprises. While the LBSN Foursquare (and its check-in offshoot Swarm) still exists, the primary function of the application has changed from being a LBSN to being a service for other digital media that is based upon the free labour of Foursquare users past and present. The value of user data has been realised in changing the function of the business from social media to big data – as Haklay (2013, p. 55) says, by breaking free into a new form. It is in these changes that value is realised, and it is in these kind of transactions and forms of commoditisation that LBSN will live on across other platforms and services.

5.3 Zombie Media

Given this political economy of LBSN and the malleability of the databases of places of POI databases that the services that developed from user-generated content, we are reticent to label LBSN as 'dead' media. 'Dead' would obviously imply no longer active but the evidence is that both the form and the data of LBSN continue to play important roles in the social and digital media environments. While there is a tendency in social media to have no appreciation of the obsolete and old, it is clear that these now relatively obscure and forgotten LBSN are still playing a role in the development of contemporary platforms. Instead of 'dead' media, we borrow from Jussi Parikka in using the term 'zombie' media (Parikka 2014, p. 131). These 'zombie' media 'haunt' the everyday, informing and helping to shape new technologies. While it might well be in the interest of technological evangelists at major social media organisations to push the 'newness' of their technologies and developments, there are always complex genealogies of the 'new' and we argue that LBSN play a very important part in the developing genealogies of social media. Indeed, as we have illustrated in this book, LBSN themselves were contingent on a complex genealogy of digital media applications and technological developments. From Lovegety and Dodgeball, to the integration of GPS in smartphones and the development of SNS, LBSN were the product of a number of technological and design advances over time. We now see that the form and function of LBSN, and the data residues of LBSN, are informing the development of other, new services and platforms. As Hjorth and Hinton (2013, p. 123) point out, far from old media being superseded by new technology a cyclical relationship of remediation (following Bolter and Grusin 2000) ensues where the evolution of technologies can be seen as generational rather than revolutionary. From our analysis of LBSN, we propose that the next generational change in LBSN is not total obsolescence but instead full integration of the most salient aspects across other social media platforms. Instead of dying out, these technologies will become ubiquitous but withdrawn and in the background. Location will no longer be special or the unique selling point of a service; it will be normal and an everyday, integrated aspect of social media use.

Huhtamo (1997; in Parikka 2015, p. 127) points out that technologies are always discursive, and they are always embedded in a larger cultural situation that demands attention if we are to understand the impact and influence of a particular technological form or artefact. The development of LBSN and the integration of LBSN cannot be considered without paying attention to the wider technological frame in which this took place. Indeed, our own research participants frequently drew attention to this when detailing their use of LBSN as part of an expectation of being (or at least being perceived as) a tech-savvy person. This technological discourse can also be seen in the development of technologies as techno-logical imaginaries, where the speculation on and design of new technol-ogies is based on reimagining current technologies for other users (Perng et al. 2016, p. 1). As Bruce Sterling (in Parikka 2015, p. 131) puts it, we are in an era of 'ghost' media where past media and technology animates and informs new technologies as part of our technological society. Whether we choose 'ghost' or our preferred 'zombie' media, it is through this positioning of LBSN in the design and futures of social and digital media that this technology lives on, and the relevance of our findings continue to resonate.

5.4   In Closing...

So, while individual LBSN applications are disappearing, their architecture and functioning are becoming stable parts of other, bigger social net-works. Through this development, there is an underlining of the impor-tance of LBSN both in a historical account of social media's incorporation of the mobile web and location, and as a historical moment of interest in social media in general. Throughout this book we have taken an implicit position that technology is not autonomous, never apart from those that use it and those that design it. Those users of LBSN that were part of our research detailed in this book and those social media engineers that have adopted parts of LBSN into other platforms illustrate the embedded nature of technology rather than a view of autonomy. It is not just technology that is shaping the modern world, but also the systems of belief that lead to technological uptake and the use of technologies in everyday life – and in the historical moment of LBSN we find these systems of belief in action in usage and design for new services. Based on this view, we argue that the findings of this book are as valid now and in the future as the time of the white heat of LBSN between 2010 and 2012.

While we have explored three main issues that we have identified in LBSN as worthy of attention – spatiality, temporality and identity – we close by emphasising that LBSN development, use and futures are all part of a cultural hermeneutics of technology that are situated across our existential lives (Ihde 1990, p. 30). What we mean here by cultural hermeneutics is a perception of the world that is a macro-perception (i.e. top level) rather than micro-perception which would be based on sensory stimulation. The micro-perceptions of technology – our handling of the device, the 'ping' of the update, the use of the application to check-in – are informed by the macro-perception of a technologically informed worldview. The relationship of these two perceptual positions is like the Gestalt figure-to-ground relationship, where perceptions of figures are influenced by the overall perceptual environment. This may seem very abstract, so we can concretise this observation: the use and effects of LBSN take place in an environment informed and shaped by social media, and the use of LBSN itself plays a role in shaping that environment. Lewis Mumford (1934/2010, p. 15) argued that the clock was the key machine of the modern age, as clock time shaped understanding of the world and ordered the activities of human beings through its representation of time. Locative media in general is beginning to become an important way of finding one's location in the world and navigating through the world, and while we are not anywhere near the status of the clock as a key technology yet the importance of these applications in shaping understanding of place for users is clear in the material we have covered in this book. As this kind of locational service becomes embedded in the very technologies and services that are already embedded into the fabric of our everyday lives, then these technologies will play a greater role in shaping the understanding of spatiality, temporality and identity for more social media and digital technology users.

As Lupton (2015, pp. 1–2) states, we interact with and are configured by the technologies that we use every day. Our embodiment of technologies is always part of an inter-relational or inter-corporeal assemblage where our usage of technologies both becomes part of our identity and is a disciplining force on us as human beings (Lupton 2013, p. 2). In a world where knowledge has been abstracted by information, location becomes a critical contextual factor in the intelligibility of this information (Tsoukas 1997, p. 872). Our use, relationship with and embeddedness within place therefore become critical to both our understanding of the world through digital media and how we might understand how others comprehend and make sense of the world through the use of this technology. While research on stand-alone LBSN might not be a red-hot topic for the future of digital media studies or post-digital theory and practice, the research we have detailed here and the research we have drawn upon in this book retains its validity as location, location-based media and the integration of location-based media become important aspects in understanding the post-digital world and understanding the everyday in this world. Take for example the very recent explosion of the 'Pokémon Go!' application. Part of the game is 'stopping' at 'Poké Stops', which are notable locations in the real world marked on the in-game map. You go to these to get items for the game, such as 'Poké Balls' that you use to catch Pokémon. This is much like the 'check-in' of LBSN apps such as Foursquare, and this activity in the 'Pokémon Go!' app brings up location specific information on local places much like the activation of an LBSN. 'Pokémon Go!'s use of an augmented reality interface as a gaming mechanism shows another emerging trajectory for these technologies, but the fundamental aspect of exploring place and gaining understanding of our environment through locative media remains much as we have argued in this book. Our use of locative applications and social media through the mobile web increasingly shapes our understanding of space, time and identity and the findings that we have outlined here act as a guide to how these critical aspects of being human in the post-digital age are mediated by social media and digital media. We see the research here as serving as a connective tissue between past and present research and future lines of enquiry. Our specific research on LBSN still matters and still will matter in the future as the salient features of LBSN become embedded and normalised across existing and new platforms. The future of social media will also be informed by existing LBSN databases and new data derived from the activities of users and their marking of location. The 'zombie' will continue to shape social media, and we must continue to pay attention to these locational aspects of social media in forming research and theory on how these applications shape our lives and our understanding of the world.

References

Albarran, A. B. (2013). *The social media industries.* London: Routledge.

Apter, M. (1991). A structural-phenomenology of play. In M. Apter & J. H. Kerr (Eds.), *Adult play: A reversal theory approach.* Amsterdam: Swets & Zeitlinger.

Arthur, W. B. (2009). *The nature of technology: What it is and how it evolves.* London: Simon and Schuster.

Barreneche, C. (2012). The order of places: Code, ontology and visibility in locative media. *Computational Culture, 2.*

Bassett, C. (2003). How many movements? In M. Bull & L. Beck (Eds.), *Auditory culture reader* (pp. 343–353). Oxford/New York: Berg.

Baudelaire, C. (1964). *The painter of modern life and other essays.* London: Phaidon Press. (Original publication 1863).

Baym, N. K. (2015). *Personal connections in the digital age.* New York: Wiley.

Beck, U., & Beck-Gernsheim, E. (2002). *Individualization: Institutionalized individualism and its social and political consequences.* London: Sage.

Belk, R. W., & Ruvio, A. A. (2013). *The Routledge companion to identity and consumption.* London: Routledge.

Benjamin, W. (1999). *The Arcades project.* (Trans. H. Eiland & K. McLaughlin.) Cambridge, MA/London: Harvard University Press. (Original work published 1927).

Berry, D. (2011). *The philosophy of software: Code and mediation in the digital age.* London: Palgrave Macmillan.

Bolter, J. D., Grusin, R., & Grusin, R. A. (2000). *Remediation: Understanding new media.* Cambridge: MIT Press.

boyd, D. (2014). *It's complicated: The social lives of networked teens.* New Haven: Yale University Press.

Boyd, J. (2005). The only gadget you'll ever need. *New Scientist, 28,* 5 March.

© The Author(s) 2017
L. Evans, M. Saker, *Location-Based Social Media,*
DOI 10.1007/978-3-319-49472-2

boyd, D., & Ellison, N. (2007). Social network sites: Definition, history, and scholarship. *Journal of Computer-Mediated Communication, 13*(1), 210–230.

Bradburne, A. (2007). *Practical rails social networking sites.* Sydney: Apress.

Bradley, A., & Armand, L. (Eds.). (2006). *Technicity.* Prague: Charles University Press.

Buchanan, I. (2000). *Michael de Certeau.* London: Sage.

Buczkowski, A. (2016). *Uber will now use Foursquare POI data to make it easier to find your destination.* http://geoawesomeness.com/uber-will-now-use-foursquare-poi-data-to-make-it-easier-to-find-your-destination/. Accessed 8 July 2016.

Butler, J. (1990). Gender Trouble, Feminist Theory, and Psychoanalytic Discourse. In L. Nicholson (Ed.), *Feminism/post-modernism* (pp. 324–340). New York: Routledge.

Caillois, R. (2001). *Man, play and games.* Chicago: University of Illinois Press. (Original work published 1958).

Campbell, S., & Kwak, N. (2011). Mobile communication and civil society: Linking patterns and places of use to engagement with others in public. *Human Communication Research, 37,* 207–222.

Campbell, S. W., & Ling, R. (2009). Effects of mobile communication. In *Media effects: Advances in theory and research* (pp. 592–606). New York: Routledge.

Chun, W. H. K. (2011). *Programmed visions: Software and memory.* Cambridge: MIT Press.

Clarke, S. (2008). Culture and identity. In T. Bennett & J. Frow (Eds.), *The Sage handbook of cultural nalysis* (pp. 510–529). London: Sage.

Cramer, H., Rost, M., & Holmquist, L. E. (2011). Performing a check-in: Emerging practices, norms and "Conflicts" in location-sharing using foursquare. In *MobileHCI 2011.* Stockholm, 30th August–2nd September, 2011.

Crawford, A., & Goggin, G. (2009). Geomobile web: Locative. Technologies and mobile media. *Australian Journal of Communication, 36*(1), 97–109.

Cunningham, C. (2013). *Social networking and impression management: Self-presentation in the digital age.* London: Rowan & Littlefield.

Dasgupta, S. (Ed.) (2013). *Studies in virtual communities, blogs, and modern social networking: Measurements, analysis, and investigations: Measurements, analysis, and investigations.* Hershey, PA: IGI Global.

De Certeau, M. (1984). *The practice of everyday life* (Trans. S. Rendell.) Berkeley and Los Angeles, CA: University of California Press.

De Lange, M., & De Waal, M. (2013). Owning the city: New media and citizen engagement in urban design. *First Monday, Special Issue "Waves Bits and Bricks: Media & the Production of Urban Space", 18,* 10.

De Souza e Silva, A., & Gordon, E. (2011). *Net locality: Why location matters in a networked world.* London: Wiley.

De Souza e Silva, A. (2006). From cyber to hybrid. *Space and Culture, 9*(3), 261–278.

de Souza e Silva, A., & Hjorth, L. (2009). Playful urban spaces: A historical approach to mobile games. *Simulation & Gaming, 40*(5), 602–625.

De Souza e Silva, A., & Frith, J. (2010). Locational privacy in public spaces: Media discourses on location-aware mobile technologies. *Communication, Culture & Critique, 3*(4), 503–525.

De Souza e Silva, A., & Sutko, D. M. (2011). Theorizing locative technologies through philosophies of the virtual. *Communication Theory, 21*(1), 23–42.

Dodge, M., & Kitchin, R. (2004). Flying through code/space: The real virtuality of air travel. *Environment and Planning A, 36*(2), 195–211.

Donath, J., & boyd, D. (2004). Public displays of connection. *BT Technology Journal, 22*(4), 71–82.

Dormehl, L. (2014). *The formula: How algorithms solve all our problems-and create more.* New York: Penguin.

Dourish, P. (2001). Seeking a foundation for context-aware computing. *Human–Computer Interaction, 16*(2–4), 229–241.

Edwards, R. (2015). *An investigation into the use of social networking sites by young people and the perceived benefits.* diplom.de.

Elden, S. (2004). *Understanding Henri Lefebvre.* London: A&C Black.

Ellison, N. (2013). Social Media and Identity. In (final project report, ed. Government Office for Science), *Future identities: Changing identities in the UK the next 10 years.* London: The Government Office for Science.

Elmer, G. (2010). Locative networking. *Aether: The Journal of Media Geography, 5*, 18–26.

Erickson, I. (2009, August 8–11). *Locative technologies and the organization of place and space.* Paper presented at the American Sociological Association Annual Conference, San Francisco, CA.

Evans, L. (2013). How to build a map for nothing: Immaterial labor and location-based social networking. In G. Lovink & M. Rasch (Eds.), *Unlike us reader: Social media monopolies and their alternatives* (pp. 189–199). Amsterdam: Institute of Network Cultures.

Evans, L. (2014). Maps as deep: Reading the code of location-based social networks. *IEEE Technology and Society Magazine, 33*(1), 73–80.

Evans, L. (2015). *Locative social media: Place in the digital age.* London: Palgrave Macmillan.

Farman, J. (2012). *Mobile interface theory: Embodied space and locative media.* New York: Routledge.

Flynn, N. (2012). *The social media handbook: Rules, policies, and best practices to successfully manage your organization's social media presence, posts, and potential.* London: Wiley.

Fortunati, L. (2002). The mobile phone: Towards new categories and social relations. *Information, Communication & Society, 5*(4), 513–528. http://dx.doi.org/10.1080/13691180208538803. Accessed 8 July 2016.

Foursquare. (2014). Foursquare. https://foursquare.com/. Accessed 1 July 2014.

Freni, D., Ruiz Vicente, C., Mascetti, S., Bettini, C., & Jensen, C. S. (2010). Preserving location and absence privacy in geo-social networks. In *Proceedings of the 19th ACM international conference on information and knowledge management* (pp. 309–318). New York: ACM.

Friedland, G., & Sommer, R. (2010). *Cybercasing the joint: On the privacy implications of geo-tagging.* Proceedings of the fifth USENIX Workshop on Hot Topics in Security (HotSec 10), Washington DC.

Frith, J. (2012). *Location – based social networks and mobility patterns: An empirical examination of how Foursquare use affects where people go.* Raleigh, NC: Pan American Mobilities Network.

Frith, J. (2013). Turning life into a game: Foursquare. *Gamification, and Personal Mobility. Mobile Media & Communication, 1*(2), 248–262.

Frith, J. (2014). Communicating through location: The understood meaning of the Foursquare check-in. *Journal of Computer-Mediated Communication*, Advance Online Publication. http://onlinelibrary.wiley.com/doi/10.1111/jcc4.12087/full. Accessed 17 February 2015.

Frith, J., & Kalin, J. (2016). Here, I used to be mobile media and practices of place-based digital memory. *Space and Culture, 19*(1), 43–55.

Fuchs, C. (2014). *Social media: A critical introduction.* London: Sage.

Gauntlett, D. (2008). *Media, gender and identity: An introduction.* London: Routledge.

Gazzard, A. (2011). Location, location, location: Collecting space and place in mobile media. *Convergence: The International Journal of Research into New Media Technologies, 17*(4), 405–417.

Geist, J. F. (1983). *Arcades: The history of a building type.* Cambridge: MIT Press.

Gibbs, S. (2016). How much are you worth to Facebook?. https://www.theguardian.com/technology/2016/jan/28/how-much-are-you-worth-to-facebook. Accessed 8 July 2016.

Giddens, A. (1991). *Modernity and self-identity: Self and society in the late modern age.* Stanford: Stanford University Press.

Gleber, A. (1999). *The art of taking a walk: Flanerie, literature, and film in Weimar culture.* Princeton: Princeton University Press.

Goffman, E. (1959). *The presentation of self in everyday life.* Garden City: Doubleday.

Goggin, G. (2013). Placing Media with mobiles. In J. Hartley, J. E. Burgess, & A. Bruns (Eds.), *A companion to new media dynamics* (pp. 202–208). Oxford: Wiley-Blackwell.

Gordon, E., Baldwin-Philippi, J., & Balestra, M. (2013). *Why we engage: How theories of human behavior contribute to our understanding of civic engagement in a digital era* (p. 21). Cambridge, MA: Berkman Center Research Publication.

Graham, S. D. (2005). Software-sorted geographies. *Progress in Human Geography*, *29*(5), 562–580.

Guha, S., & Birnholtz, J. (2013). Can you see me now? location, visibility and the management of impressions on foursquare. In *Proceedings of the 15th international conference on human-computer interaction with mobile devices and services* (pp. 183–192). New York: ACM.

Haklay, M. M. (2013). Neogeography and the delusion of democratisation. *Environment and Planning A*, *45*(1), 55–69.

Hampton, K. N., Livio, O., & Sessions Goulet, L. (2010). The social life of wireless urban spaces: Internet use, social networks, and the public realm. *Journal of Communication*, *60*(4), 701–722.

Haraway, D. (Ed.) (1991). A cyborg manifesto: Science, technology, and socialist-feminism in the late twentieth century. In *Cyborgs and Women: The Reinvention of Nature* (pp. 149–181). New York: Routledge.

Haraway, D. (2004). *The Haraway reader*. New York: Routledge.

Heidegger, M. (1962). *Being and time*. Oxford: Wiley-Blackwell.

Heidegger, M. (1977). *The question concerning technology and other essays* (Trans. M. Heim.) New York: Harper & Row.

Heidegger, M. (2012). *Contributions to philosophy (of the event)*. Indianapolis: Indiana University Press.

Hinton, S., & Hjorth, L. (2013). *Understanding social media*. Sydney: Sage.

Hjorth, L. (2008). Being real in the mobile reel: A case study on convergent mobile media as new media and a sense of place. *Convergence*, *14*(1), 91–104.

Hjorth, L. (2012). Mobile relocations: A case study of locative media in Seoul. *Convergence Journal*. doi: 10.1177/1354856512462360.

Hjorth, L., & Richardson, I. (2014). *Gaming in social, locative and mobile media*. London: Palgrave MacMillan.

Hogan, B. (2010). The presentation of self in the age of social media: Distinguishing performances and exhibitions online. *Bulletin of Science, Technology, & Society*, *30*(6), 377–386.

Hoskins, A. (2011). Media, memory, metaphor: Remembering and the connective turn. *Parallax*, *17*(4), 19–31.

House, N. V., & Churchill, E. F. (2008). Technologies of memory: Key issues and critical perspectives. *Memory Studies*, *1*, 295.

Hughes, T. P. (1983). *Networks of power: Electrification in western society, 1880–1930*. New York: The Johns Hopkins University Press.

Huhtamo, E. (1997). From kaleidoscomaniac to cybernerd: Notes toward an archaeology of the media. *Leonardo*, *30*(3), 221–224.

Huizinga, J. H. (1992). *Homo Ludens: A study of the play-element in culture.* London: Beacon Press. (Original work published 1938).

Humphreys, L.. (2005). Cellphones in public: Social interactions in a wireless era. *New Media & Society, 7*(6), 810–833.

Humphreys, L.. (2007). Mobile social networks and social practice: A case study of Dodgeball. *Journal of Computer-Mediated Communication, 13*(1), 341–360.

Humphreys, L.. (2008). Mobile devices and social networking. In M. Hartmann, P. Rossler, & J. R. Hoflich (Eds.), *After the mobile phone* (pp. 115–130). Berlin: Frank & Timme.

Humphreys, L.. (2010). Mobile social networks and urban public space. *New Media & Society, 12* (5), 763–778.

Humphreys, L.. (2013). Mobile social media: Future challenges and opportunities. *Mobile Media & Communication, 1*(1), 20–25.

Humphreys, L.., & Liao, T. (2013). Foursquare and the parochialization of public space. *First Monday, 18,* 11.

Ihde, D. (1990). *Technology and the lifeworld: From garden to earth (No. 560).* Indianapolis: Indiana University Press.

Ihde, D. (1993). *Postphenomenology: Essays in the postmodern context.* Evanston, IL.: Northwestern University Press.

Issa, T., Isaias, P., & Kommers, P. (Eds.) (2015). *Social networking and education: Global perspectives.* London: Palgrave Macmilan.

Iwatani, Y. (1998). Love: Japanese style. *Wired News.* http://archive.wired.com/culture/lifestyle/news/1998/06/12899. Accessed 4 November 2016.

Joffe, B. (2007). Mogi. In F. Borries, S. P. Walz, & M. Böttger (Eds.), *Space time play* (pp. 224–225). Basel: Birkhäuser.

Kalin, J., & Frith, J. (2016). Wearing the City: Memory P (a) laces, smartphones, and the rhetorical invention of embodied space. *Rhetoric Society Quarterly, 46*(3), 222–235.

Kellner, D. (1992). Popular culture and the construction of postmodern identities. In S. Lash & J. Friedman (Eds.), *Modernity and Identity* (pp. 141–178). Wiley: London.

Kelsey, T. (2010). *Social networking spaces: From Facebook to Twitter and everything in between.* Sydney: Apress.

Kitchin, R. (2014). *The data revolution: Big data, open data, data infrastructures and their consequences.* Sage: London.

Kitchin, R., & Dodge, M. (2011). *Code/space: Software and everyday life.* Cambridge: MIT Press.

Korzybski, A. (1931, December 28). *A non-Aristotelian system and its necessity for rigour in mathematics and physics.* Paper presented before the American Mathematical Society at the New Orleans meeting of the American Association for the Advancement of Science. Reprinted in Science and Sanity, 1933, pp. 747–761.

Lash, S., & Friedman, J. (1992). *Modernity and identity*. London: Wiley.

Lefebvre, H. (1947). *Descartes*. Paris: Editions Hier et Aujourd'hui.

Lefebvre, H. (1991). *The production of space*. Blackwell: Oxford. (Originally published 1974).

Levinas, E. (1987). *Time and the other and additional essays*. Pittsburgh: Duquesne University Press.

Lewis, M. (2014). *Flash boys: A Wall Street revolt*. New York: W.W. Norton and Co.

Li, E. Y. (Ed.), (2013). *Organizations and social networking: Utilizing social media to engage consumers: Utilizing social media to engage consumers*. Hershey, PA: IGI Global.

Licoppe, C. (2004). 'Connected' presence: The emergence of a new repertoire for managing social relationships in a changing communication technoscape. *Environment and Planning D: Society and Space, 22*(1), 135–156.

Licoppe, C., & Inada, Y. (2008). Geolocalized technologies, location-aware communities, and personal territories: The Mogi case. *Journal of Urban Technology, 15*(3), 5–24.

Light, B. (2014). *Disconnecting with social networking sites*. London: Palgrave Macmillan.

Lindqvist, J., Cranshaw, J., Wiese, J., Hong, J., & Zimmerman, J. (2011). I'm the mayor of my house: Examining why people use foursquare-a social-driven location sharing application. In *Proceedings of the SIGCHI conference on human factors in computing systems* (pp. 2409–2418). New York: ACM.

Ling, R. (2004). *The mobile connection: The cell phones impact on society*. San Francisco, CA: Morgan Kaufmann.

Ling, R., & Pederson, P. E. (2005). *Mobile communications: Re-negotiation of the social sphere*. London: Palgrave Macmillan.

Ling, R., & Horst, H. A. (2011). Mobile communication in the global south. *New Media & Society, 13*(3), 363–374.

Ling, R., & Yttri, B. (2002). Hyper-coordination via mobile phones in Norway. In J. Katz & M. Aakhus (Eds.), *Perpetual contact: Mobile communication, private talk, public performance* (pp. 139–169). New York: Cambridge University Press.

Lipschultz, J. H. (2014). *Social media communication: Concepts, practices, data, law and ethics*. New York: Routledge.

Livingstone, S. (2008). Taking risky opportunities in youthful content creation: Teenagers' use of social networking sites for intimacy, privacy and self-expression. *New Media & Society, 10*(3), 393–411.

Lofland, L. H. (1998). *The public realm: Exploring the city's quintessential social territory*. London: Transaction Publishers.

Lupton, D. (2013). Quantifying the body: Monitoring and measuring health in the age of mHealth technologies. *Critical Public Health, 23*(4), 393–403.

Lupton, D. (2015). *Digital bodies*. SSRN 2606467. https://ssrn.com/abstract= 2606467 or http://dx.doi.org/10.2139/ssrn.2606467. Accessed 6 December 2016.

MacColl, I., & Richardson, I. (2008). A cultural somatics of mobile media and urban screens: Wiffiti and the IWALL prototype. *Journal of Urban Technology*, 15, Issue 3 December 2008, 99–116.

Mackenzie, A. (2003). Transduction: Invention, innovation and collective life. http://www.lancs.ac.uk/staff/mackenza/papers/transduction.pdf. Accessed 8 July 2016.

Mallia, G. (Ed.), (2013). *The social classroom: Integrating social network use in education: Integrating social network use in education*. Hershey, PA: IGI Global.

Mandiberg, M. (2012). *The social media reader*. New York: NYU Press.

Manning, P. (1992). *Erving Goffman and modern sociology*. London: Polity Press.

Martin, J. A. (2014). Mobile media and political participation: Defining and developing an emerging field. *Mobile Media and Communication*, 2, 173–195.

Marwick, A. (2013). *Status update: Celebrity, publicity, and branding in the social media age*. New Haven: Yale University Press.

Mendelson, A. L., & Papacharissi, Z. (2010). Look at us: Collective narcissism in college student Facebook photo galleries. In Z. Papacharissi (Ed.), *The networked self: Identity, community and culture on social network sites* (pp. 1–37). London: Routledge.

Merleau-Ponty, M. (1962). *Phenomenology of perception*. London: Routledge and Kegan Paul.

Merleau-Ponty, M. (1964). *Signs*. Evanston, IL: Northwestern University Press.

Merrin, W. (2014). The rise of the gadget and hyperludic media. *Cultural Politics*, 10(1), 1–20.

Michael, M. G., & Michael, K. (2009). *Uberveillance: Microchipping people and the assault on privacy*. http://ro.uow.edu.au/infopapers/711. Accessed 8 July 2016.

Milani, L., Bramilla, F., & Confalonieri, E. (2014). "What does it mean? What can I do?" Social networks and identity experimentation in adolescence. *Qwerty*, 2, 30–50.

Milne, E. (2010). *Letters, postcards, email: Technologies of presence*. New York: Routledge.

Moores, S. (2006). Media uses and everyday environmental experiences: A positive critique of phenomenological geography. *Particip@tions*, 3(2), 233–256.

Mumford, L. (1934/2010). *Technics and civilization*. Chicago, IL: University of Chicago Press.

Murphie, A., & Potts, J. (2003). *Culture and technology*. Basingstoke: Palgrave Macmillan.

Nagy, P., & Neff, G. (2015). Imagined affordance: Reconstructing a keyword for communication theory. *Social Media+ Society*, 1(2), 10.1177/2056305115603385.

Nieuwdorp, E. (2005). *The pervasive interface: Tracing the magic circle*. Paper presented at the DiGRA 2005 Conference: Changing Views: Worlds in Play, Vancouver, British Columbia, Canada.

November, V., Camacho-Hübner, E., & Latour, B. (2010). Entering a risky territory: Space in the age of digital navigation. *Environment and planning D: Society and space, 28*(4), 581–599.

Obee, J. (2012). *Social networking: The ultimate teen guide (vol. 32)*. Los Angeles: Scarecrow Press.

Okazaki, S., & Mendez, F. (2013). Exploring convenience in mobile commerce: Moderating effects of gender. *Computers in Human Behavior, 29*(3), 1234–1242.

Papacharissi, Z. (2011). A networked self. In Z. Papacharissi (Ed.), *The networked self: Identity, community and culture on social network sites* (pp. 304). London: Routledge.

Parikka, J. (2012). *What is media archaeology?*. Cambridge: Polity Press.

Parikka, J. (2014). 21st century theory: A new yesterday. *Spike, 41.*

Parikka, J. (2015). Media archaeology: Questioning the new in media arts. *Akbanksanat and Amber Festival*. http://postdigital.amberplatform.org/? cat=94. Accessed 8 July 2016.

Partridge, K. (Ed.), (2011). *Social networking*. New York: HW Wilson.

Pasquale, F. (2014). *The black box society: The secret algorithms that control money and information*. Cambridge: Harvard University Press.

Pătruţ, B., & Pătruţ, M. (Eds.) (2014). *Social media in politics: Case studies on the political power of social media*, Vol. 13. London: Palgrave Macmillan.

Peachey, A., & Childs, M. (Eds.) (2011). *Reinventing ourselves: Contemporary concepts of identity in virtual worlds*. Amsterdam: Springer Science & Business Media.

Perng, S.-Y., Kitchin, R., & Evans, L. (2016). Locative media and data-driven computing experiments. *Big Data & Society, 3*(1), 1–12. January–June.

Rainie, H., Rainie, L., & Wellman, B. (2012). *Networked: The new social operating system*. Cambridge: MIT Press.

Reuters, I. (1998). Bleep at first sight. *Wired*. http://archive.wired.com/culture/ lifestyle/news/1998/05/12342. Accessed 8 July 2016.

Richardson, I. (2005). Mobility, new social intensities and the coordinates of digital networks. *Fibreculture, 6.*

Richardson, I. (2007). Pocket technoscapes: The bodily incorporation of mobile media. *Continuum: Journal of Media & Cultural Studies, 21*(2), 205–216.

Richardson, I., & Wilken, R. (2009). Haptic vision, footwork, place-making: A peripatetic phenomenology of the mobile phone pedestrian. *Second Nature: International Journal of Creative Media, 1*(2), 22–41.

Ryan, P. K. (2011). *Social networking*. New York: The Rosen Publishing Group.

Saker, M. (2016). Foursquare and identity: Checking-in and presenting the self through location. *New Media & Society.* doi: 10.1177/1461444815625936.

Saker, M., & Evans, L. (2016a). Everyday life and locative play: An exploration of Foursquare and playful engagements with space and place. *Media, Culture & Society.* doi: 10.1177/0163443716643149.

Saker, M., & Evans, L. (2016b). Locative mobile media and time: Foursquare and technological memory. *First Monday, 21,* 2.

Salen, K., & Zimmerman, E. (2004). *Rules of play: Game design fundamentals.* Cambridge, MA: MIT.

Sample, J. T., & Ioup, E. (2010). *Tile-based geospatial information systems: Principles and practices.* Amsterdam: Springer Science & Business Media.

Schmalz, D. L., Colistra, C. M., & Evans, K. E. (2015). Social media sites as a means of coping with a threatened social identity, in *Leisure sciences. An Interdisciplinary Journal, 37*(1), 20–38.

Schwartz, R., & Halegoua, G. R. (2014). The spatial self: Location-based identity performance on social media. *New Media & Society,* doi: 10.1177/ 1461444814531364.

Senft, T. (2012). Micro-celebrity and the Branded Self. In J. Hartley, J. Burgess, & A. B. Blackwell (Eds.), *A companion to new media dynamics.* Malden, MA: Wiley- Blackwell Aslinger, B. S.

Shah, S. (2016). Twitter and Foursquare partner to let you follow major events through location tags. http://www.digitaltrends.com/social-media/twitter-foursquare-location/. Accessed 8 July 2016.

Shields, R. (1994). Fancy footwork: Walter Benjamin's notes on *flânerie.* In K. Tester (Ed.), *The Flâneur.* London: Routledge.

Siapera, E. (2012). *Understanding new media.* London: Sage.

Siegert, B. (2011). The map is the territory. *Radical Philosophy, 169,* 13–16.

Simmel, G., & Wolff, K. H. (1950). *The sociology of Georg Simmel.* New York: Simon and Schuster.

Smythe, D. W. (1977). Communications: Blindspot of western Marxism. *CTheory, 1*(3), 1–27.

Soja, E. W. (1996). *Thirdspace: Journeys to Los Angeles and other real-and-imagined places.* London: Wiley.

Sotamaa, O. (2002). All the world's a Botfighters stage: Notes on location-based multiuser gaming. In F. Mäyrä (Ed.), *Proceedings of computer games and digital cultures conference* (pp. 35–44). Tampere, Finland: Tampere University Press.

Statista. (2016). Statistics and facts about Facebook. https://www.statista.com/ topics/751/facebook/. Accessed 11 April 2016.

Stiegler, B. (1998). *Technics and time, 1: The fault of Epimetheus.* Stanford: Stanford University Press.

Tester, K. (1994). *The Flâneur.* London: Routledge.

Thrift, N., & French, S. (2002). The automatic production of space. *Transactions of the institute of British geographers*, 27(3), 309–335.

Tian, K., & Belk, R. W. (2005). Extended self and possessions in the workplace. *Journal of Consumer Research*, 32(2), 297–310.

Tsoukas, H. (1997). The tyranny of light. *Futures*, 29(9), 827–843. doi: 10.1016/s0016-3287(97)00035-9.

Turkle, S. (1996). Parallel lives: Working on identity in virtual space. In D. Grodin & T. R. Lindlof (Eds.), *Constructing the self in a mediated world: Inquiries in social construction* (pp. 156–175). Thousand Oaks, CA: Sage.

Urry, J. (2002). *Sociology beyond societies: Mobilities for the twenty-first century*. London: Routledge.

Van Dijck, J. (2009). Mediated memories as amalgamations of mind, matter, and culture. In R. Van Der Vall & R. Zwijnenberg (Eds.), *The body within* (pp. 157–172). Brill: Amsterdam.

Van Dijck, J. (2011). Flickr and the culture of connectivity: Sharing views, experiences, memories. *Memory Studies*, 4, 401.

Virilio, P. (1997). *Open sky*. New York: Verso.

We Are Social (2016) Digital in 2016. http://wearesocial.com/uk/special-reports/digital-in-2016. Accessed 8 July 2016.

Weber, J., & Novet, J. (2015) Foursquare by the numbers: 60 M registered users, 50 M MAUs, and 75 M tips to date. *VentureBeat*. http://venturebeat.com/2015/08/18/foursquare-by-the-numbers-60m-registered-users-50m-maus-and-75m-tips-to-date/. Accessed 8 July 2016.

Week, T. (2015). No, Yelp isn't actually suing *South Park*. http://theweek.com/speedreads/584442/no-yelp-isnt-actually-suing-south-park. Accessed 8 July 2016.

White, E. (2008). *The Flaneur: A stroll through the paradoxes of Paris*. London: Bloomsbury.

Wilde, S. (2012). *Viral marketing within social networking sites*. Berlin: Diplomica Verlag GmbH.

Wilken, R. (2008). Mobilizing place: Mobile media, peripatetics, and the renegotiation of urban places'. *Journal of Urban Technology*, 15(3), 39–55.

Wilken, R. (2011). Bonds and bridges: Mobile phone use and social capital debates. In R. Ling & S. Campbell (Eds.), *Mobile communication: Bringing us together or tearing us apart* (pp. 127–151). London: Transaction Publishers.

Wilken, R. (2012). Locative Media: From specialized preoccupation to mainstream fascination. *Convergence*, 18, 243–247.

Wilken, R., & Goggin, G. (2012). *Mobile technology and place*. New York: Routledge.

Wilken, R., & Goggin, G. (2014). *Locative media*. London: Routledge.

INDEX

© The Author(s) 2017
L. Evans, M. Saker, *Location-Based Social Media*,
DOI 10.1007/978-3-319-49472-2

Printed in the United States
By Bookmasters